MALNUTRITION AND
INTELLECTUAL DEVELOPMENT

MALNUTRITION AND INTELLECTUAL DEVELOPMENT

Edited by

JOHN D. LLOYD-STILL

Publishing Sciences Group, Inc.
Littleton, Massachusetts
a subsidiary of the CHC Corporation

Published in USA by
Publishing Sciences Group, Inc.
545 Great Road
Littleton, Massachusetts 01460

ISBN 0–88416–181–1

Printed in Great Britain

Contents

List of contributors

H. Peter Chase, M.D., Associate Professor of Pediatrics, University of Colorado Medical Center, 4200 East Ninth Avenue, Denver, Colorado 80220, U.S.A.

Gordon P. Harper, M.D., Research Fellow Child Psychiatry, Judge Baker Guidance Center and Department of Psychiatry, Children's Hospital Medical Center, 300 Longwood Avenue, Boston, Massachusetts 02115, U.S.A.

Irving Hurwitz, Ph.D., Assistant Professor Psychology, Harvard Medical School, Children's Hospital Medical Center, 300 Longwood Avenue, Boston, Massachusetts 02115, U.S.A.

John D. Lloyd-Still, M.B., M.R.C.P., D.C.H., Associate Professor of Pediatrics, Northwestern University, Head Division of Gastroenterology, Director Cystic Fibrosis Center, Children's Memorial Hospital, 2300 Children's Plaza, Chicago, Illinois 60614, U.S.A.

Carolyn Moore Newberger, M.Ed., Psychologist, Judge Baker Guidance Center, 295 Longwood Avenue, Boston, Massachusetts 02115, U.S.A.

Eli H. Newberger, M.D., Director Family Development Study, Children's Hospital Medical Center, 300 Longwood Avenue, Boston, Massachusetts 02115, U.S.A.

Zena A. Stein, M.D., Director Epidemiology of Mental Retardation Research Unit, New York State Department Mental Hygiene, Professor Division of Epidemiology, School of Public Health, Columbia University, 600 West 168th Street, New York, New York 10032, U.S.A.

Mervyn Susser, M.B., B.Ch., Professor and Chairman Division Epidemiology, School of Public Health and Administrative Medicine, Columbia University, 600 West 168th Street, New York, New York 10032, U.S.A.

CHAPTER 1

Introduction

JOHN D. LLOYD-STILL

Two major preventable diseases are of great importance in influencing both the physical and psychological status of child health in the world today. The largest numerically is that of malnutrition; the World Health Organization estimates that there are at least 100 000 000 children in the world suffering from malnutrition[1]. Fetal and early childhood under-nutrition, an extensive man-made scourge within our power to avoid, does indeed play a demonstrable part, interdependently with a host of other environmental factors which are its common accompaniment, in permanently reducing many a human being's achievement to a level below his/her naturally endowed potential[2]. The second major prevent-able problem in child health is the result of child abuse and neglect and occurs predominantly in developed countries. The incidence of this condition varies between 60 000 to 500 000 cases per year in the U.S.A. Physical abuse is a greater killer of infants between 6 and 12 months of age than any specific cancer, malformation or infectious disease, and from 1–6 months of age it is second only to the Sudden Infant Death Syndrome. After one year of age it is the second greatest cause of death after true accidents[3]. Failure to thrive accounts for 5% of hospital admissions under 2 years of age in many areas of the U.S.A. Moreover, neglect and failure to thrive are the commonest cause of malnutrition in developed countries.

The stimulus for this monograph arose in response to Valman's article on intelligence after malnutrition caused by neonatal resections of the ileum[4]. A letter was written to the editor of the *Lancet* pointing out that similar findings had been shown in studies of infants with cystic fibrosis and other gastrointestinal disorders who had undergone a period of severe malnutrition during infancy[5]. It was noted that the present status of the effects of malnutrition on the intellectual develop-

ment of the human was still controversial despite an extensive bibliography extending over two decades. Some of the numerous reasons for
this confusion are detailed in this monograph. Many of these difficulties
stem from extrapolating the findings on the effects of malnutrition in
animal models to the human and the important variables of critical
periods of vulnerability of the brain together with species differences.
Although there is no doubt that the majority of studies on malnourished
populations demonstrate a significant decrease in intellectual functioning on follow-up, the important influence of the social and environmental factors inherent in a study of malnourished populations from
developing countries must be taken into account.

We designed an approach to this dilemma by inviting contributions
from a number of different specialists involved with this problem and
asking them to review the data in their specific area of expertise with
particular reference to the human rather than the animal model. The
first chapter is written by Dr Chase, who is a pediatrician, nutritionist
and basic scientist, and whose research has involved studying the effects
of malnutrition on the various constituents of the brain. His review
'Undernutrition and Growth and Development of the Human Brain' is
largely concerned with the data that is known on the effects of malnutrition on the human brain, much of it the result of his own experiments and observations. He stresses that it is impossible to separate
nutritional from other environmental factors influencing intelligence in
the human, and discusses some of the many biochemical structural
alterations that could be associated with impaired brain structure. These
include loss of certain types or of total numbers of brain cells, impaired
myelin formation, reduced cell size or numbers of axon–dendritic connections, and impairment of neurotransmission due to other damage
that we are unable to measure in the present status of knowledge. He
discusses the effects of intrauterine and postnatal undernutrition on
brain cells, myelin, brain protein and dendritic axonal connections and
cell size. His conclusions explain the importance of loss of neuronal cells
in utero and of glial cells in postnatal life, but questions the importance
to intelligence of the loss of glial cells in the cerebellum following postnatal malnutrition, as has been found in laboratory animal models. Dr
Chase believes that optimal postnatal care would be expected to correct
any deficiencies resulting from the delay in myelin formation in infants
suffering from intrauterine malnutrition, and emphasizes that we do

not yet know whether the diminution in myelin lipids secondary to post-natal undernutrition is irreversible. Studies on the protein content of the brain showed similar effects. The data on axon–dendritic connections is far more difficult to interpret.

The next chapter on 'Prenatal Nutrition and Mental Competence' is written by Drs Stein and Susser, who are epidemiologists specializing in the study of malnourished populations and the epidemiology of mental deficiency. Their book on the effects of the Dutch famine 1944–1945[6] is a classic in its field, and they have drawn on this data extensively for their review. They stress the difficulties in separating entirely the experiences of malnutrition in the prenatal period from those of the postnatal period. Studies of twins point indirectly to effects of intrauterine malnutrition on intelligence. Many studies suggest that low birth weight is an antecedent of reduced mental competence, and the lower the birth weight, the greater the mental handicap tends to be. All these observations taken together show that poor nutrition, low birth weight and mental retardation are associated under certain conditions. As they conclude, 'The simplest assumption is that poor maternal nutrition causes low birth weight, and that low birth weight leads to brain impairment and mental retardation. But the nature of the links is far from clear.' They go on to discuss how, among the complex of variables associated with social class, differences between families and not birth weight differences between individuals are the likely intervening link between social environment and measured intelligence. The distinction between organic impairment and dysfunction may be at the root of the apparent incoherence of the relationship of mental performance with low birth weight. Many factors that limit or enhance function and influence level of disability act postnatally. Some studies, but not all, point to interaction between the effects of low birth weight and social class to produce mental retardation. In these studies moderately low birth weight was associated with mild mental retardation or lowered intelligence quotient only among the lower classes and not among the higher.

In their studies of the Dutch famine, Stein and Susser found that below a certain nutritional threshold the fetus is vulnerable to some extent in the third trimester of gestation in terms of intrauterine growth and early postnatal mortality. Of the fetal dimensions reported, weight has seemed most sensitive to nutritional effects, and length and head size less sensitive. They believe that prenatal brain cell depletion in fetuses exposed during the third trimester to maternal starvation probably occurred. If it occurred this outcome points to great resilience on the part of the surviving fetuses, for organic impairment did not become manifest in this function. Moreover, among adult survivors they found no evidence that prenatal nutrition affected mental competence. Finally, they believe that poor prenatal nutrition cannot be considered a factor in the social distribution of mental competence among surviving adults in industrial societies. They state that this does not exclude a possible factor effect of prenatal nutritional deprivation in combination with poor postnatal nutrition, especially in pre-industrial societies, but the data is not yet available. They believe that one must look to the effects of postnatal nutritional deprivation in severely malnourished populations to seek out the possible effects of nutrition on mental competence.

Before discussing the studies on the effects of postnatal malnutrition on intellectual functioning, we have a contribution by Dr Hurwitz, a clinical psychologist specializing in the assessment of mental competence in the infant, pre-school and school age child. When investigating the effects of malnutrition on intelligence, it is essential to understand about intelligence tests, what parameters a specific test measures, its limitations, applicability and relevance to the study of intellectual functioning, and whether abnormal findings on tests of intelligence in the pre-school child really have any relevance to the intellectual competence of the adult. This subject is by no means as simple as it may appear and improvements in intellectual functioning from a stimulatory programme for deprived infants and pre-school children can demonstrate dramatic improvement in intellectual quotient that deteriorates on prolonged follow-up into the school years[7]. Dr Hurwitz discusses the advantages and disadvantages of the various tests of intellectual development and gives us an authoritative critique with which to approach some of the results of the studies which we have to interpret.

Dr Lloyd-Still is a pediatrician with a special interest in the nutritional and gastrointestinal diseases of children. He reviews the clinical studies on the effects of malnutrition during infancy on subsequent physical and intellectual development. For this review, 13 well-controlled studies of malnourished populations were selected from different parts of the world. The data from all these studies were then compared in terms of the multiple variables that could affect a study on this population.

Consistently lacking in most of these studies is information on prenatal factors, birth weight and the IQ of the parents. The problems of socio-economic deprivation are again emphasized. The important influence of the duration of hospitalization on the future intellectual development of the infant is discussed. This subject has been neglected by most investigators, and further analysis of this variable shows significant difference between various groups in whom reduced performance on intellectual testing was all ascribed to poor nutrition. The lack of prospective longitudinal studies is stressed, as is the inability to come to many definite conclusions. Controversial findings include some of the new data from developed countries that have failed to show permanent deficits in intellectual functioning although less serious deficits in fine motor co-ordination have been observed. These findings of impairment of fine motor function raise the question whether these are not the human counterpart of the experimental studies in animals demonstrating the particular vulnerability of the cerebellum to nutritional insult. Lloyd-Still also discusses the possibility that some of the findings of cerebral atrophy and poor intellectual functioning which are present in some individuals despite adequate recovery from malnutrition as measured by anthropometric parameters could be a manifestation of the child abuse-neglect syndrome.

The next chapter by the Drs Newberger and Harper approaches the problems of malnutrition, poor social functioning and neglect from a different perspective. The authors are child development specialists with a particular interest and expertise in the development and inter-relationships of infants, children and their families and the sequelae that deficits in family function have on the development of the child. They discuss the evidence that shows how the problems of failure to thrive, child abuse and neglect may result in malnutrition and poor performance in tests of intellectual functioning. In other words, identical findings of low intellectual functioning such as is seen in malnourished populations in developing countries, can be produced in developed countries by a disturbance in the family relationship.

Their chapter on 'The Social Ecology of Malnutrition in Childhood' focuses on the settings in which malnutrition occurs in order to provide a framework for the organization and understanding of the complex ecological context of malnutrition. The authors have designed a model for conceptualizing the major elements of the nutritional ecology and their relationship at different levels of analysis. In the first level of analysis they discuss the implications of 'global' malnutrition, such as weather, soil, energy, fertilizer, resources, prices and population and point out the difficult moral choice we shall all have to face in the future. The second level of analysis concerns the social, political and economic order in a given country and thus the availability of food to family units. The third level of analysis discussed is family functioning and the stress, distribution patterns, food beliefs, parental maturity and family size, and the family's ability to get food to the child. The most obvious example of this situation is the condition of 'failure to thrive' where the infant presents with nutritional failure. This is one of the group of childhood disorders sometimes referred to as the 'pediatric social illnesses' which also include accidents, poisonings, child neglect and abuse. Newberger *et al.* produce data from their family development study, a large controlled descriptive epidemiological inquiry into the postulated common origins of the pediatric social illnesses which shows significantly more parameters of stress in the mother's childhood and the lack of social support in the 'failure to thrive' group. They postulate that failure to thrive may be a nutritional consequence of determinants stemming from earlier parental life experience and a contemporary familial reality and a given family's capacity to cope with these realities. In the level 3 analysis, an understanding of how the family organizes itself around food and feeding is critical to an understanding of many nutritional problems. Operating on the family ecology rather than exclusively on the nutrition of the child is often essential to effect enduring nutritional change.

At the level 4 analysis of the social ecology of malnutrition in childhood, the child's own contribution to his nutritional function is considered. Examples are given of how individual children may respond to interpersonal, physical and inner psychological stress, particularly during developmentally vulnerable periods of ego integration by compromising their own nutritional intake. Moreover, each individual's adaptation needs to be understood in the family context.

The model defined in this chapter fosters understanding of the many causal elements determining malnutrition at different levels of the social scale and can help to identify points of entry to effect change and the necessary scope of intervention at each point. This chapter raises many controversial issues and explains why it is so difficult to isolate and interpret the effects of malnutrition on intellectual functioning.

Basic research in animals is essential to delineate the effects of malnutrition on brain structure and function, and Dr Chase has pointed out how much of this information will always lack correlation with the human model. A word of warning is necessary, however, before we become overwhelmed with the plethora of reports on the devastating results of malnutrition on brain function. Account must be taken of the remarkable resilience and adaptation of the human species. The literature contains examples of many reports on this subject that have been misrepresented. A recent article showing that prenatal zinc deficiency altered the behaviour pattern of the adult rat[8] is of interest for zinc is essential for the normal development of the brain. The hypothesis was then expounded that fetuses of women who consume inadequate amounts of zinc during pregnancy may be at risk for intrauterine brain development and body growth, and that the changes caused by these factors may be persistent and be manifest as mental retardation. Another study demonstrated that rats given hydroxyurea, an inhibitor of cell division, at the beginning of the period of neurogenesis (14 days) showed a severe reduction in postnatal whole brain weight (by 31–33%) and made more errors in the Hebb–Williams Maze test[9]. The authors speculated that the large number of moderately retarded children whose handicap is without known aetiology may have suffered a similar early loss of neurons, and if so this preparation could provide a useful animal model.

The cytomegalovirus is the commonest known microbiological cause of brain damage in infancy and its effect on neuronal multiplication results in microcephaly and mental retardation[10]. Moreover, we have the technical means to study the incidence of this disease, and the results show that numerically even the cytomegalovirus accounts for a very small proportion of the total retarded population. However, postnatal traumas, such as subdural haematomas and head injuries resulting from the physical abuse of infants, are far more important numerically as a cause of microcephaly and retardation. Both retrospective studies of microcephalic populations[11] and prospective studies of large series of battered children[3] have demonstrated that this area seems likely to be one of the leading causes of mental retardation where the aetiology has been previously labelled unknown. Due attention should be paid to the subject of child abuse and neglect, for we now have the means to prevent child abuse and to rehabilitate 80% of this group of families[12]. It is hoped that this monograph will influence the perspective of future investigators so that the facts that are known may be clarified, and remedies applied to these areas when available. Hypotheses such as prenatal zinc deficiency in the mother or the injection of unnatural substances like hydroxyurea during pregnancy leading to mental retardation are experimental and speculative and must not be misinterpreted in their application. Emphasis needs to be placed on those areas where the scientific facts are conclusive.

Further caution on the effects of malnutrition upon brain development and behaviour is necessary as a result of the findings reported by Drs Heath, Harlow and Prescott[13]. Preliminary data obtained from a small group of isolation raised macaca Rhesus monkeys are the first evidence that aberrant electrophysiological activity occurs in deep cerebellar nuclei as well as in other deep vein structures in association with severely disturbed behaviour resulting from maternal social deprivation. The five male Rhesus monkeys were selected because they were severe self-biters and all had diverse early experiences ranging from semi-inadequate to extremely inadequate. The differences in early rearing conditions and behavioural abnormalities in these animals parallel the differences in the electrophysiological brain activity. The two monkeys who were separated from their mothers at birth and reared separately thereafter showed the most severe brain abnormalities. These findings support the point of view that variation in early social sensory experiences in the developing infant have profound effects upon the developing brain and behaviour which may or may not be reversible and would clearly interact with any nutritional deficiencies experienced during early development. Furthermore, the cerebellum appears to be unusually sensitive to the early insult of maternal social deprivation as well as to the effects of malnutrition. These findings also suggest the difficulties that may be encountered in obtaining electrophysiological characteristics from clinical analysis of the data that uniquely reflects the effects of malnutrition separately from those of isolation rearing (sensory deprivation) and, more importantly, their interaction.

Most of the data discussed in this monograph concerns overall IQ assessments and Dr Hurowitz has warned us of the fallacy of using this single measurement of intelligence. Klein *et al.*, have recently reported on the effects of starvation in infancy (pyloric stenosis) on subsequent learning abilities[14]. The authors refer to a previous study[15] of army conscripts who had pyloric stenosis in infancy who were followed up in terms of physical and intellectual development, where the IQ on follow-up failed to show significant differences between the malnourished and control groups. Klein *et al.* studied a group of fifty subjects aged 5–14 years who had pyloric stenosis and compared them to forty-four siblings and fifty matched controls. Socio-economic deprivation was not present. Learning ability was negatively correlated with the degree of severity of the starvation. Starvation resulting in a reduction of more than 10% of the expected body weight in infancy was associated with poorer learning abilities, especially those involving short-term memory and attention span. However, despite exclusion of premature infants, social problems and neurologically abnormal children, there are other factors that could still operate as variables. Moreover, the more severe the dehydration, the more likely is the development of cortical vein thrombosis. Furthermore, the more severely malnourished infants would also tend to be hospitalized the longest. Although this study cannot isolate malnutrition from other variables the results have important implications if they are confirmed.

One question which arises is whether lack of any particular nutriment is more likely than any other to produce the effects on brain growth and intellectual development. Whether the dietary deficit may be one of mere quantity of food, or one specifically of protein, a particular amino acid, a range of essential fatty acids, iron, zinc or folic acid, it is an attractive unifying hypothesis that the final common path feature bearing on the developing brain is the growth restriction that all these dietary deficits may produce[16]. Such a unifying hypothesis admits into the aetiology of poor brain growth all the non-nutritional and secondary nutritional growth retarding conditions providing they operate on the growth programme for a substantial part of the brain growth spurt period.

We must be constantly aware that advances in medical technology may result in unknown effects on the developing human brain. Phenylketonuria results in mental retardation unless treatment with a low phenylalanine diet is instituted when a decrease in the incidence of the mental retardation can be demonstrated[17]. However, incorrect dietary treatment of phenylketonuria may lead to iatrogenic malnutrition and lowered IQ levels[18]. The increasingly widespread practice of supplying the nutritional requirements of premature infants by intravenous alimentation is known to result in high levels of certain amino acids in the blood. At present we have little knowledge of the effects that these temporarily elevated levels of amino acids may have on the future development of the infant human brain[19].

Lastly we would hope that this monograph would stimulate further discussion of some of the many issues raised and ultimately our ability to remedy some of the devastating effects that can ensue from malnutrition. It is fitting here to pay tribute to Dr Cicely Williams for not only being the first to describe Kwashiorkor but for her extraordinarily far-sighted solutions to the problems of protein calorie malnutrition. In the Blackfan lecture at Harvard in 1973[20] on health services in the home she summarized some of these responsibilities. She quoted Sir James Spence that there are 3 factors that destroy and damage child life. Deficiencies in food and environment, deprivation of maternal and family care, and dependence on outside assistance[21]. We can do no better than to refer to the writings of Dr Cicely Williams for the answers to some of the problems that have been posed by this monograph.

REFERENCES

1. Bengoa, J. M. (1974). The Problem of Malnutrition. *W.H.O. Chron.*, **28**, 3
2. Dobbing, J. (1974). The later growth of the brain and its vulnerability. *Pediatrics*, **53**, 2
3. Schmitt, B. D. and Kempe, C. H. (1975). The pediatricians role in child abuse and neglect. *Current Problems Pediatrics*, **5**, 2
4. Valman, H. B. (1974). Intelligence after malnutrition caused by neonatal resection of ileum. *Lancet*, **i**, 425
5. Lloyd-Still, J. D. and Schwachman, H. (1974). Intelligence after malnutrition. *Lancet*, **i**, 679
6. Stein, Z. M., Susser, M., Saenger, G. and Marolla, F. (1975). *Famine and Human Development: The Dutch Hunger Winter of 1944–45.* (New York: Oxford University Press)
7. Clarke, A. D. B. and Clarke, A. M. (1974). Mental retardation and behavioural change. *Br. Med. Bull.*, **30**, 179
8. Halas, E. S. and Sandstead, H. H. (1975). Some effects of prenatal zinc deficiency on behaviour of the adult rat. *Pediatr. Res.*, **9**, 94
9. Adlard, B. P. F. and Dobbing, J. (1975). Maze learning by adult rats after inhibition of neuronal multiplication in utero. *Pediatr. Res.*, **9**, 139
10. Stern, H., Elek, S. D., Booth, J. C. and Fleck, D. G. (1969). Microbial causes of mental retardation. The role of prenatal infections with cytomegalo virus, rubella virus and toxoplasma. *Lancet*, **ii**, 443

11. Oliver, J. E. (1975). Microcephaly following baby battering and shaking. *Br. Med. J.*, **2**, 262

12. Kempe, C. H. and Helfer, R. E. (1972). *Helping the Battered Child and His Family*. (Philadelphia: J. B. Lippincott Co.)

13. Heath, R. G. (1975). Maternal-social deprivation and abnormal brain development: disorders of emotional and social behaviour. In *Brain Function and Malnutrition* (J. W. Prescott, M. S. Read and D. B. Coursin editors.) p. 295 (New York: John Wiley and Sons)

14. Klein, P. S., Forbes, G. B. and Nader, P. R. (1975). Effects of starvation in infancy (pyloric stenosis) on subsequent learning abilities. *J. Pediatr.*, **87**, 8

15. Berglund, G. and Rabo, E. (1973). A long-term follow-up investigation of patients with hypertrophic pyloric stenosis—with special reference to the physical and mental development. *Acta Pediatr. Scand.*, **62**, 125

16. Dobbing, J. (1974). The later development of the brain and its vulnerability. In *Scientific Foundations of Pediatrics* (J. A. Davis and J. Dobbing editors.) p. 565 (Philadelphia: W. B. Saunders Co.)

17. Dobson, J., Koch, R., Williamson, M., Spector, R., Frankenberg, W., O'Flynn, M., Warner, R. and Hudson, F. (1968). Cognitive development and dietary therapy in phenylketonuric children. *N. Engl. J. Med.*, **278**, 1142

18. Hanley, W. B., Linsao, L., Davidson, W. and Moes, C. A. F. (1970). Malnutrition with early treatment of phenylketonuria. *Pediatr. Res.*, **4**, 318

19. Raiha, N. C. R. (1974). Biochemical basis for nutritional management of preterm infants. *Pediatrics*, **53**, 147

20. Williams, C. D. (1973). Health services in the home. *Pediatrics*, **52**, 773

21. Spence, J. C., Walton, W. S. and Miller, F. J. (1954). *1,000 Families in Newcastle on Tyne* (London: Oxford Medical Publishers)

CHAPTER 2

Undernutrition and growth and development of the human brain

H. Peter Chase

INTRODUCTION

It is now generally accepted that intelligence is related to genetic intellectual potential as well as to environmental factors. Intelligence is in itself hard to define, and as a quantitative measurement is influenced by variables such as motivation and attention span which are possibly altered in previously undernourished children. Figure 2.1 illustrates

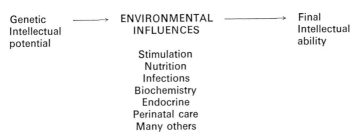

Figure 2.1. Many 'internal' and 'external' influences occur with undernutrition that can influence brain development and intellectual testing. As it is impossible to separate nutrition as a single factor, the term 'environutritional deprivation' is suggested.

some of the environmental factors currently believed to influence intelligence. Nutrition is one of these factors, but is so closely intertwined with 'internal' and 'external' influences on intelligence that it will never be completely separated as a single entity. Potentially harmful 'internal' alterations refer to changes within the body, such as in biochemical or endocrine homeostasis or infections (see below), which might alter normal brain development. External influences outside the body would include factors such as parental stimulation which are partially measurable. The environment that leads to undernutrition is usually lacking in many important types of infant stimulation. The undernourished infant is apathetic and irritable which contributes to his not being stimulated, but also to his not attaining stimulation from the environment himself. Intrauterine life is more apt to be deprived in undernourished populations, with as many as 40% of newborn infants weighing under 2501 g[1]. This is related to a higher incidence of prematurity as well as of small-for-date infants, both of which result in a greater incidence of neonatal problems, and both of which influence later intelligence. Intrauterine and postnatal infections occur more frequently in undernourished children, and IgM levels, suggesting fetal exposure to infection, may be elevated in 20% of the newborns in preindustrial societies[1]. Intrauterine infections as well as postnatal infections, can affect the brain. Biochemical disarrangements, such as hypernatremia (resulting from diarrhea) or hypoglycaemia (resulting from low birth weight or other causes) occur more frequently in undernourished children and can also impair normal brain development. Endocrine dysfunction, such as hypothyroidism, is associated with poor mental development, and low serum thyroxine levels are found with undernutrition[2]. The clinical importance of this is as yet unknown. It must thus be realized that, as emphasized previously[3], separating nutrition *per se* from other factors influencing intelligence is impossible in the human. However, attempts to do so will continue to be made, and various percentages will be assigned to undernutrition as an inhibiting influence on intelligence in comparison with other environmental factors. It is probably wiser to choose new terminology, such as environmental–nutritional or 'environutritional' deprivation rather than to carry on with such terms as 'nutritional-deprivation' in referring to the large numbers of undernourished children in the world's population.

Having dispelled the idea of nutrition alone as having a definable detrimental influence on human intelligence, it would now be nice to proceed to discuss the human brain biochemical alterations resulting from environutritional insults which lead to impaired intelligence. Unfortunately, this is also not simple, as we do not know which factors in the brain are important to intelligence. It is apparent that brain structure as related to intelligence and neurological integrity, is, to borrow a word from the geneticists, 'multifactorial'. Thus, there are many biochemical–structural alterations that could be associated with impaired brain function. Some of these include: loss of certain types or of total numbers of brain cells, impaired myelin formation, altered protein synthesis, altered glycosaminoglycan (mucopolysaccharide) formation, reduced cell size or number of axon–dendritic connections, impairment of formation of neurotransmitters, and other changes that we are not yet even capable of considering. Evidence for and against alterations of some of these factors being important in the under-nourished brain will be discussed. Brain weight is obviously a composite of many subparts, and will not be separately discussed in this review. Emphasis will be placed on the data currently available pertaining to the human brain following both intrauterine and postnatal undernutrition. This is done with the realization that animal experiments have generally been experimentally 'cleaner', and that it is unlikely that any two humans would ever have similar genetic, nutritional, stimulatory, infectious or other environmental influences to allow them to be considered together in an experimental group. In addition, available human specimens are of necessity from non-survivors and results are representative of the extremes. However, the differences in timing of brain development between experimental animals and the human, and their dissimilarity in intellectual functioning, warrant the consideration of current human data in detail, apart from the many studies using laboratory animals.

BRAIN CELLS

NORMAL DEVELOPMENT

A reduction in the total number of cells, in the cell composition, or the loss of a specific type of cell might be important in altering brain function. Nutritional insults might cause any of these, depending on the time of the insult. The concept of 'critical time periods' in organ development has received much attention in the last half century, and refers to a period of rapid development which cannot occur again at a later time period. The 'critical period' in brain development varies in timing between species and for various brain subparts, but would come between early fetal life and the fourth postnatal year for the human

(Figure 2.2). It must be admitted that the choice of the fourth year as a cut off is as yet poorly defined. However, clinical evidence, such as the discontinuation of the low-phenylalanine diet in children with phenyl-ketonuria, suggests that insults after 4 years of age are unlikely to

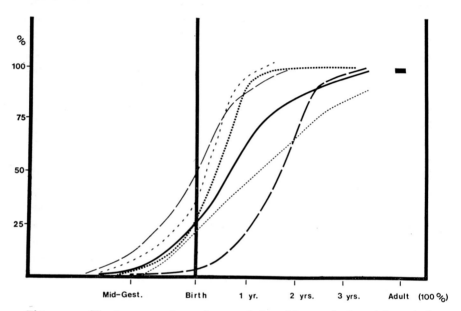

Figure 2.2 The important times of accumulation of human brain weight and of biochemical constituents are shown. Some components, such as myelin lipid, are later in accumulation than other components, such as glycosaminoglycans. Thus, an earlier insult (e.g. intrauterine) might have a greater effect on glycosaminoglycans, whereas a later insult (e.g. postweaning) might have a greater effect on myelin lipid accumulation in the human brain, (total brain weight ———— , total myelin lipid — —, total cells ·········, total protein ···········, total NANA - - - - -, total glyco-saminoglycans — —).

permanently impair further brain development. There is, however, some gradual increase in brain weight after age 4 years, and some increase in head circumference until approximately age 18 years[4].

Within an organ as diverse in makeup as the brain, it is known that critical periods exist for individual parts. Thus, in early development the neuronal crest must properly close by the end of the first fetal month or it may never close, resulting in a myelomeningocele or other permanent defects. Neuronal cells have been thought by microscopists, and more recently by neurochemists using computer analysis of DNA data[5], to form primarily *in utero* in the human. Glial cells, in contrast, form primarily in the first year of postnatal life. Myelin, as will be discussed later, accumulates primarily in the second postnatal year in the human. Thus, an insult during one period of development may affect one brain parameter more than another. It is essential to understand the normal periods of development within an organ in order to appreciate the effects of the timing of any insult on that organ.

Total cell number is usually estimated biochemically by measuring total DNA. This is valid assuming a constant amount of DNA per cell nucleus, which is true for most brain cells. The Purkinje cells in the cerebellum are polyploid, with varying amounts of DNA per cell nucleus, but these are relatively few so that they do not preclude the use of DNA to represent cell number.

Figure 2.2 shows the normal period of brain cell formation in the human brain. Approximately 25% of the adult number of total brain cells are present at birth, 66% by age 6 months, and 90–95% by age 1 year[5-7].

It is uncertain when the final few per cent of brain cells form, but this is probably by age 3 years. Thus, the first year following birth is the time period in which the greatest percentage of cells develop. Although the cortex and brain stem accumulate cells at a similar time, with approximately 54% present at birth, the cerebellum is slower in onset with only 29% of cells present at birth, but reaches its total cell number prior to other brain areas[5, 8]. With this shorter, more rapid period of cell multiplication, occurring during the vulnerable postnatal life, it might be suspected to be more susceptible to injury. This seems to be the case.

The mature human brain has about 30% of all cells present in the cerebellum, 68% in the cerebrum and 2% in the brain stem. In the newborn infant the cerebellum has only 18% of all brain cells, but the proportion increases with the rapid growth of the cerebellum in the first four months after birth to the adult 30% level. It is important to remember that there are species differences in the numbers of cells in the various brain areas as well as differences in the timing of cell formation. Thus, the adult rat brain has 46% of cells in the cerebellum, 43% in the cerebrum, and 11% in the brain stem. These differences in comparison with human brain reflect the greater development of the human cerebral cortex.

EFFECTS OF INTRAUTERINE UNDERNUTRITION

If the time period for formation of neuronal cells is primarily *in utero*, it is obviously important to consider whether nutritional insults at this time alter cell formation. Intrauterine undernutrition is most marked following placental failure to deliver adequate nutrients to the fetus, as occurs with most small-for-gestational-age (SGA) infants. It is less marked following poor maternal diets, depending in part upon maternal stores, which depend on past and present maternal food intake, illnesses, and the number and frequency of past pregnancies.

Results are available from two studies of brain development in SGA infants[9, 10] (Figure 2.3). In the first of these, total DNA, representing

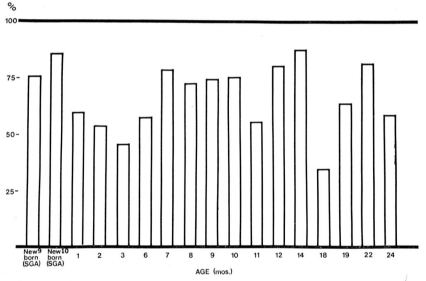

Figure 2.3 All human brain total DNA values found in the literature [9–10, 13, 15] for which control and malnourished pairs of a similar age were available are included. Control and undernourished values were paired only if the infants were within 0.5 months of age for infants under age 6 months, or within 1 month of age for infants over 6 months. The value for the control member of the pair was set at 100% for each pair. The age of the pair is shown on the abscissa. The newborn values represent more than one infant.[9, 10]

total cell number, was 19% lower in the cerebrum–brain stem fractions of SGA infants compared with term appropriate weight for gestational age (AGA) infants ($p > 0.05$), and cerebellum DNA was 35% lower

($p < 0.02$). In the latter study[10], differences in body weight were not as marked as in the earlier study, and the mean body weight of control infants (2875 g) was somewhat low (normal mean birth weight in U.S. $= 3400$ g). DNA content was reduced by 11, 15 and 20% in the cerebellum, cerebrum and brain stem respectively, of the low birth weight infants, although differences were statistically significant ($p < 0.05$) only for the cerebrum.

As 10% of all newborn infants are SGA by definition[11], it is probable that some reduction in brain cell number occurs *in utero* in a large number of human infants. With adequate postnatal rehabilitation, it is likely that recovery might occur during the period of postnatal cell division. This recovery has been demonstrated using an experimental animal (the guinea-pig) even more mature in brain development than the human at birth[12], but recovery will not ever be possible to study adequately in the human. It should, of course, be remembered that brain forming postnatally to make up for an intrauterine insult may not be of the same type (e.g. neurons *v.* glial) as those forming prenatally.

EFFECTS OF POSTNATAL UNDERNUTRITION

There has been much publicity in recent years in both the scientific and lay literature concerning a reduction in numbers of brain cells as a result of postnatal malnutrition. In reality, as discussed in the Introduction, this is only one of many brain alterations that might be important, and there is no reason to equate its importance to intelligence with any greater certainty than any of the other possible alterations. We also do not know how many neurons or other cells are required for optimal function, and it is likely an excess may exist in the normal brain.

There have been reports from two laboratories to date of brain DNA levels in children dying following postnatal malnutrition. Figure 2.3 represents total brain DNA data from some of these infants for whom a value was also available on a closely age-matched control infant. In the first study, Winick and Rosso[13] described results from nine children succumbing to malnutrition in Chile. Three of the infants weighed under 2000 g at birth, and had a reduction in brain DNA of over 50% when they died between ages 2 weeks and 6 months. This is a considerably greater reduction than occurs in the laboratory animal undernourished to the greatest extreme possible, and raises the question what other environmental insults might have been present. At a minimum the infants were of low birth weight and had a combined intrauterine insult, shown above to also reduce brain DNA. The other six infants had a reduction in brain DNA of approximately 20%. As only total brain DNA was measured, it is not known if this reduction was primarily in the cerebellum. Birth weights of the other six infants were not given so it is unknown if they were also small at birth. None of the nine infants was breast fed and their major source of food was a liquid made of flour and water. The clinical picture was that of 'severe infantile marasmus', and although serum protein levels were not reported, it might be suspected that at least some of them had marasmic-kwashiorkor. In a second report from the same group[14] the effects of infantile mal-nutrition on DNA levels was studied in the cerebellum, cerebrum and brain stem in nine infants from Chile and seven from Jamaica all of whom were 'severely malnourished during the first year of life'. All showed 'severe third degree malnutrition' and died between ages 1.3 and 24 months. Total DNA levels were reduced in all malnourished infants in approximately equal proportions in all three brain areas, the cerebrum, cerebellum and brain stem.

In a report from a second laboratory of the effects of malnutrition on human brain cellularity[15], the infants were all initially breast fed and birth weights were known to be normal for 4 of the 6 infants. Four infants were marasmic and two marasmic-kwashiorkor, and all died between ages 1 and 2 years. Cerebrum–brain stem DNA was reduced by 10% in the brains from the undernourished infants and cerebellum DNA was not altered. Statistically significant differences in brain DNA were not found in comparison with control specimens for either the cerebellum or the cerebrum–brain stem. This is the more frequent type of malnutrition affecting the masses of the world's undernourished children. Initial nutrition is adequate with breast feeding, but declines as the maternal milk supply becomes inadequate and other protein foods of good quality are unavailable. The reasons for the disparity in results between the two laboratories is most likely in the timing of the onset of the malnutrition, which in the first study began at or before birth, and in the latter study began after an initially adequate period of breast feeding. Perhaps the differences in results of these two studies should give emphasis to the importance of encouraging breast feeding in the world's pre-industrial societies.

In addition to the reduction in number of cells, the types of cells affected following postnatal malnutrition should be considered. As noted above, it is likely that human neuronal cells are primarily formed *in utero*, and glial cells in postnatal life. Following intrauterine undernutrition, cellularity was primarily reduced in the cerebellum[9]. In addition, the work in laboratory animals has shown postnatal malnutrition to primarily reduce cell number in the cerebellum, where there are large numbers of glial cells. The importance of the loss of the glial supporting cells to intelligence would not be anticipated to be as great as the loss of neuronal cells, which would be more likely to occur *in utero*. The loss of cerebellar cells, would likewise not be expected to be as detrimental as the loss of cells in the cerebrum. Poseidonios thought the cerebellum the centre of memory in A.D. 300[18]. However, complete cerebellum removal in fish, amphibians, reptiles, birds, cats, dogs and man in the past two centuries has shown disorders of movement, while 'no recognizable functions related to vital processes, intellect, perception or the sensory functions of touch, sight, or hearing seemed disturbed by its removal'[18]. The importance to intelligence of the loss of glial cells in the cerebellum following postnatal malnutrition, as has been found in laboratory animal models, would have to be questioned.

MYELIN

NORMAL DEVELOPMENT

Myelin sheaths cover many of the axons in the central and peripheral nervous system, and are important in the insulation of nerve fibres, in the protection of the nerve fibres from extraneous molecules including water, and for their influence on the velocity of transmission of the nerve impulses. Myelin is formed from supporting cells, oligodendroglia, in the central nervous system. It extends on the axon from near the cell body to a point close to the end of the axon. It is laid down over the axon in concentric lamellae (Figure 2.4), and its deposition results in the 'white matter' of brain, in contrast to the 'grey matter' in areas in which nerve fibres do not have myelin around them.

Myelin is made up of 80% lipid (dry weight), and contains approximately 50% of the lipid in the brain. Cerebroside and cerebroside sulphate (sulphatide) are characteristic 'myelin lipids', in that they are

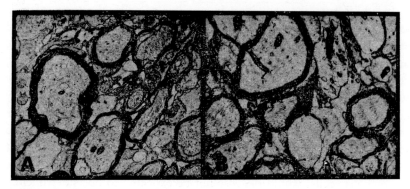

Figure 2.4 Electron photomicrograph ($\times 3500$) of myelin from a normal (A) and undernourished (B) brain showing the concentric layers of myelin around the central axons. No consistent qualitative differences in gross structure were found as a result of undernutrition.

found in higher concentration in myelin than in other brain parts. Cholesterol is found in high content in myelin, but is not specific for this membrane and is also found in high content in other brain membranes. It is laid down in the human brain before there is any histological evidence of myelination[19]. It is thus incorrect to use it as a biochemical indicator of myelination, although this has frequently been done.

There are believed to be two metabolic pools of myelin, one being a consistent slowly turning over pool which is formed early in development, and the other a rapidly exchanging pool which remains active in adult life. The physiological significance of this latter pool is not yet understood. The alterations associated with a loss of myelin in diseases such as multiple sclerosis and the lipodystrophies support the fact that myelin is essential to neurological integrity.

Myelin accounts for a large percentage of brain weight (greater than 25%) and accumulates over a relatively short period in early brain development. Once again, understanding the normal period of development is necessary in order to evaluate the effects of intrauterine and postnatal undernutrition on myelin formation. It can be seen (Figure 2.2) that over 50% of cerebroside–sulphatide, used as an index of myelination, accumulates between ages 12 and 24 months and formation is probably complete prior to age 4 years. Only a small fraction is present at birth, although the percent increase in the perinatal period is large. Per cent increase refers to the increase over a time period compared with the baseline starting level, and is misleading as one starts from very low levels. It will not show the period in which the greatest quantity of myelin (or any material) is being formed. The total quantity of cerebroside–sulphatide at 34 weeks gestation is under 50 uM, with a 300–400% increase to 160 uM at term. This is a large percent increase, but still represents only a very small fraction of the adult quantity of myelin. However, this early period of formation may be important in later myelination. Evidence for this comes from animal experiments, in which rats undernourished from birth and then rehabilitated at the start of the active period of myelination (age 10 days) did not show later recovery of a maximal rate of sulphatide formation or of the quantity of cerebroside[20, 21].

EFFECTS OF INTRAUTERINE UNDERNUTRITION

The studies to date evaluating the effect of intrauterine undernutrition on brain development are the same two studies[9, 10] referred to in the above section on cellularity. In the earlier study[9] the total cerebroside–sulphatide content of brain stem–cerebrum analysed together was approximately 50% lower in low birth weight infants compared with AGA infants ($p < 0.01$). The ratio of cholesterol to cerebroside–sulphatide was used as an index of myelination. As cholesterol levels are similar in most membranes and cerebroside–sulphatide levels are low in non-myelin membranes, the ratio of the two lipids is higher in non-myelin membranes or in the very early stages of myelination. Although the ratios were high in both AGA (49) and SGA (79) brains, the higher index in the SGA brains confirmed a delayed state of myelin formation. The activity of the enzyme believed to be rate-limiting in sulphatide formation, galactolipid sulphotransferase, was uniformly low in the SGA brains (as in preterm infants) and was considerably higher in the brains of the AGA infants.

In the second study of SGA infants[10], the glycolipid ('galactose–cerebroside') was 35% lower in the medulla oblongata and 27% lower in the cerebrum of the low birth weight infants. The values varied considerably and were not statistically different ($p > 0.05$), although differences in total lipid content were found ($p < 0.02$). Once again the 'normal' infants were lower in birth weight (2875 g) than in the earlier study (3417 g).

In summary, although it is likely that a slight delay in myelin development is at such an early stage that optimal postnatal care would be anticipated to correct any deficiencies, it will be impossible ever to adequately evaluate recovery in the human. However, animal studies[12], using a species (the guinea-pig) more mature in brain development at birth than the human in which postnatal correction would be less likely than in the human, have shown complete postnatal recovery of cerebroside–sulphatide levels following a 33% reduction ($p < 0.01$) at birth resulting from intrauterine undernutrition.

EFFECTS OF POSTNATAL UNDERNUTRITION

Whereas intrauterine undernutrition has been defined to exist in 10% of newborn infants[11], 50% of the world's children in the 1960s were estimated to suffer from some degree of undernutrition in postnatal life[22]. Because myelin develops almost entirely in the postnatal period, and it is one of the few brain parameters for which alteration is known to be associated with loss of neurological integrity (see above) it is particularly important in relation to postnatal undernutrition.

Three studies to date have reported brain lipid determinations in undernourished human infants[15, 23, 24]. In the first of these, Fishman *et al.*[23] analysed white matter dissected from the frontal lobe of four undernourished Puerto Rican children and two control children, all of whom died of dehydration and diarrhea. The two undernourished infants who had an age matched control were 4 and 12 months old, so that they died prior to the time of the majority of myelin being formed (12 to 24 months, Figure 2.2). Although statistical comparisons were not possible, the cholesterol concentrations were identical in the white matter of the control and undernourished infants of both pairs. The glycolipid levels in the white matter of the undernourished children were 27 and 19% lower in the 6- and 12-month-old pairs respectively, and plasmologen levels were 20 and 15% lower. These results do not give information pertaining to the total brain quantities of lipids, but suggest instead that either the myelin in the dissected white matter of the malnourished infants had an abnormal lipid composition, or more likely, that less myelin was present in the white matter. Data was expressed as per cent dry weight which should correct for differences in brain water content secondary to the malnutrition or varying degrees of dehydration. It would, however, be helpful to know the variability in lipid composition of white matter dissected from similar areas of brains from control infants of a similar age. No two brains are identical, and the normal variability in number of nerve fibres, nerve endings or heavier myelinated tracts would presumably alter the composition of the dissected white matter to some extent even between control specimens. It was also not possible to evaluate lipid deposition in the undernourished infants with increasing age (e.g. per gram brain), as data was presented only for white matter and only as per cent of dry weight. Birth weights were low for the three undernourished infants for which this information was available, and as noted above, would have an effect particularly at ages 2 and 4 months.

In a second study of brains from Chilean infants[24], specimens from six undernourished infants ages 1–9 months, and three infants dying between ages 12 and 17 months, and from controls were analysed for cholesterol and lipid phosphorous. The samples studied consisted of 5 mm slices composed of a mixture of white and grey matter located anterior and posterior to the central sulcus. Total lipid to DNA ratios were expressed for the control and undernourished infants, showing similar results in the infants under age 1 year, and a marked reduction in the brains of the three undernourished infants who were over age 1 year. It is not stated, but presumably the total lipid refers to all brain lipid rather than just cholesterol and phospholipid. Both cholesterol and phospholipid were also much lower in the slices of the three older undernourished children when expressed as total per brain. It should be remembered that the brain is not homogeneous, and the quantity of lipid (or of DNA) in the area of the brain sliced may not be similar to the lipid content in the remainder of the brain, so that conversion to total brain lipid must be done with caution. The authors concluded 'myelin content as reflected by total lipid or cholesterol or phospholipid is also reduced in proportion to DNA in the first year of life'. As discussed above, neither total phospholipid nor cholesterol are specific for myelin, although it would be unlikely to get this much change in these two lipids without having myelin affected. The time of onset of undernutrition in these children was not given. However, understanding the normal period of myelin lipid formation with the greatest accumulation between 12 and 24 months, the finding of greater alteration in the three older children is not surprising.

In the third study of brain lipids following postnatal undernutrition[15], total cerebrums and brain stems from six Guatemalan infants with malnutrition and five controls, all dying between ages 12 and 24 months, were analysed for total lipid, cholesterol, cerebroside, sulphatide, phospholipid and ganglioside. As noted above in the section on brain cellularity, these infants were breast fed and had normal nutrition in early life, as with the majority of the world's undernourished children. Total brain levels of cerebroside, sulphatide, cholesterol and phospholipid and total lipid were all statistically reduced ($p < 0.05$) in the malnourished specimens of age matched pairs. The concentrations of the myelin lipids cerebroside and sulphatide were also reduced ($p < 0.02$) when expressed in mg of lipid per g dry lipid weight, although the concentrations of the other lipids similarly expressed were not statistically altered. This suggests that 'myelin lipids' are reduced to a greater extent than lipids found in other brain membranes. The molar ratios of cholesterol to cerebroside–sulphatide were again used as an index of myelin maturation, where lower levels indicate greater maturation. The index for the control brains was 1.24 and for the test brains 1.55. Both values were considerably lower than the value (see above) of 49 found in normal infants at birth, indicating that considerable maturation from birth had occurred. Once again, these findings are not unexpected realizing that the undernutrition was most marked during the period of greatest myelin formation.

In summary, it appears that postnatal undernutrition in the second year of life diminishes the formation of myelin lipids. We cannot state whether these alterations are irrevocable, although further studies of brains from children having undernutrition between age 12 and 24 months, and dying of other causes at later ages may eventually answer this question. Animal studies to date[20, 21, 25] suggest that the likelihood for complete recovery is not good.

BRAIN PROTEIN

NORMAL DEVELOPMENT

Protein is of obvious importance in all tissues, particularly in the forms of enzymes, hormones, transport molecules within cells, and membrane structures (including myelin). In its membraneous capacity it is present with lipids in all subcellular membranes as well as in cell walls, and thus contributes to the regulation of the flow of ions and metabolites between subcellular structures as well as between cells. Consideration of a 'critical period' in brain protein formation is difficult, as many proteins are being formed continually throughout life and alterations occur even within the diurnal variation of a single day. In adult experimental animals, the average half-life of brain proteins based on glucose carbon incorpoation studies is between 10 and 20 days[26]. Human brain protein is constantly turning over also, and thus must be considered differently to, for example, cells which reach a relatively constant stable population. The bulk of brain protein and the measurements considered in this section pertain primarily to structural protein. The initial period of human brain protein accumulation is longer than that of either cell division or myelin formation, although it is not yet well defined. The quantities of brain protein accumulated are thought to be linear from the sixth month *in utero* to the second postnatal year, and the rate probably then falls off somewhat (Figure 2.2).

Protein formation is directed by RNA (in turn mediated by DNA) and one theory of memory attributes changes in RNA bases and protein as being fundamental to memory[27].RNA in the brain consists primarily of ribosomal RNA, which is predominantly located in neuronal cells[28]. Unfortunately, even the total brain RNA levels measured to date in control and malnourished children are likely only estimates due to the instability of RNA after death, particularly in postmortems performed as long as 24 hours later. For this reason, only brain protein, and not RNA, will be considered in this review.

EFFECTS OF INTRAUTERINE UNDERNUTRITION

The major quantity of human brain protein at birth is in the cerebrum (92%) compared with about 6% in the cerebellum and 2% in the brain stem. In both studies done to date of the biochemical composition of the brains of term SGA and AGA infants[8,9], statistically significant differences were not found in the total protein content of the cerebrum and brain stem. Both studies described statistically significant reductions in total protein in the cerebellum, but this was related to the overall decrease in cerebellar weight, and protein expressed per gram wet weight of tissue or per mg DNA was not reduced. The 12% reduction[9] and 18% reduction[10] in total brain protein in the SGA brains is represented graphically in Figure 2.5. It can be concluded that at least the bulk of total brain protein, located in the cerebrum, is not altered quantitatively by intrauterine undernutrition.

The activity of only one enzyme, galactolipid sulphotransferase, has been evaluated in SGA and AGA brains[9]. This enzyme is important in sulphatide formation for myelin, and was markedly reduced in the SGA brains. It is likely that activities of other enzyme-proteins may also be lower in the less mature brains of SGA infants. Thus, although the total quantity of cerebrum protein is not altered as a result of intrauterine undernutrition, there may be qualitative changes. These could be related to enzyme protein formation or activation, hormonal imbalance, or other factors and do not imply a specific quantitative reduction in enzyme protein. It is most likely that the described changes would be only temporary and would return to normal with good postnatal nutrition.

EFFECTS OF POSTNATAL UNDERNUTRITION

Two laboratories have reported total brain protein data from children dying with postnatal undernutrition[13-15]. The values from all undernourished infants for whom an age-matched control was available are shown in Figure 2.5 and demonstrate a consistent reduction, although varying quantitatively, in total brain protein in the brains from undernourished children. In the first of the three studies[13], as noted above under Brain Cells, three of the nine undernourished infants likely suffered from at least combined intrauterine deprivation. In the brains from two of these three infants and from a fourth infant, the protein levels were approximately 7 g, compared with levels of between 20 and 30 g in control infants. This reduction of 70–80% is considerably greater than occurs with undernutrition alone in any experimental animal model. The other infants had reductions of approximately 50% compared with the control of nearest age. In a second study from the same laboratory[14] the total protein results were somewhat variable, with a 3-month undernourished (test) infant having a cerebrum level of 15.3 g and a control infant a level of 18.8 g. An 8-month-old test infant had a level of 50 g whereas two 9-month-old controls had levels

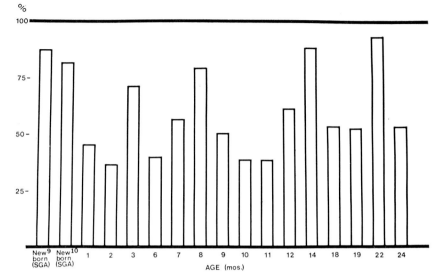

Figure 2.5 All human brain total protein values found in the literature[9, 10, 13–15] for which control and malnourished pairs of a similar age were available are included. The samples and age pairing are the same as in Figure 2.3.

of 46 and 81 g. A 14-month-old control had a protein value of 78 g whereas 15- and 17-month-old test infants had levels of 72 and 39 g respectively. An 18-month-old control had a level of 64 g whereas an 18-month-old test infant had a level of 70 g, and a 22-month-old test infant a level of 34 g. Part of the variation in the undernourished infants may have been related to the unknowns of (i) the time of onset, and (ii) the severity over an unknown time period of the undernutrition, as well as (iii) not knowing the degree of dietary protein deficiency in the 'marasmic' infants. It is apparent, however, that this group also gets lower protein levels in brains of normal infants in the first month after birth (9–12 g) compared with the two studies cited above under Intrauterine Undernutrition where term neonates had cerebrum protein levels of 14–20 g. These lower neonatal levels and the variability, particularly between control infants where total values at 10, 14, 18 and 24 months were 86, 78, 64 and 92 g respectively[14], may be related to not initially doing an alkaline hydrolysis under heat to break down protein–lipid complexes, which do not otherwise react normally with the method for protein analysis used. Values for controls between the two studies from the same laboratory also show poor agreement, with the levels of 40.0 and 49.1 g at $8\frac{1}{2}$ and $11\frac{1}{2}$ months for whole brain protein in the initial study, and levels of 80.7 and 86.1 g at 9 and 10 months respectively for cerebrum (only) protein in the second study.

In the third study of brain protein values of postnatally under-nourished children[15], the infants all died between ages 12 and 24 months after being initially breast fed (see above, Brain Cells) and the clinical protein status was more clearly defined. Brain protein concentrations (per g wet weight or per mg DNA) were similar in the cerebrum–brain stem and cerebellum for brains from control and test children. Total protein values were also statistically similar ($p > 0.05$) for under-nourished (46.3 ± 12.2 g) compared with control (55.3 ± 10.4 g) infants. Total cerebellum protein was lower ($p < 0.05$) in test (4.5 ± 0.7 g) compared with control (5.4 ± 0.7 g) children mainly due to differences in cerebellum weights. The quantities of protein found in control brains in this study were in line with the first rather than the second report from the previous laboratory.

These studies suggest that postnatal malnutrition in the first year of life results in a reduction in brain protein levels, but that this reduction is less when the malnutrition occurs after initial breast feeding. The ten infants under age 1 year in Figure 2.5 had a mean total brain protein reduction in comparison with age-matched controls of 48%, compared with the infants over 1 year who had a mean reduction of 31%. The reduction in the 1- to 2-year-old children described in the third study[15] was greater than for DNA, but less than for myelin lipids.

DENDRITIC-AXONAL CONNECTIONS AND CELL SIZE

NORMAL DEVELOPMENT

Histological studies[29] have shown that the dendrites and axons make up approximately 50% of the volume of the brain, with neuronal cell bodies constituting about 4%, and glial cells and myelin the remainder. Cell size would be a useful measurement if we could assume it related to dendritic–axon alterations, particularly in the cerebrum. This is probably true when studying a specific layer and/or region of the brain, as in the microchemical studies of Bass *et al.*[30] but it certainly does not apply for the usual determinations for whole brain. Cell size is probably more meaningful as a cerebellar measurement, where it gives an estimate of cell body size of the large numbers of glial cells. As studies of cerebrum and brain stem cell size in the human have reported means for the entire areas to date, the results are probably meaningless and certainly not a reflection of axon–dendritic arborization.

The methods of measuring axon–dendritic terminals (neuropils) are twofold, neither of which are very satisfactory. The first consists of biochemical measurements, and the second of histological measurements. Recent work from the laboratories of Svennerholm and others, as reviewed by Svennerholm[31], has shown that gangliosides were not distributed within neurons as initially thought, but were actually found primarily at nerve endings and can thus be used as an estimate of the numbers of nerve endings. Gangliosides are complex lipids containing *N*-acetyl neuraminic acid (NANA) and have achieved their greatest notoriety through their excessive accumulation in Tay Sachs Disease. Their exact function is unknown, but may be related to ion transport or neurotransmitter storage or release. It has been suggested that they accumulate in the human brain from the second prenatal month to the second or third postnatal month[31]. However, their maximal quantitative formation occurs following birth. We obtained values of 223 ± 58 mg total brain *N*-acetyl neuraminic acid (representative of ganglioside) in normal newborn infants[9] and levels of approximately 700 mg at ages 1–2 years[15]. Their 'critical period' of formation (Figure 2.2) occurs prior to that of glial cell division, myelin formation, or protein formation, and the rate of formation is likely very rapid in the highly susceptible postnatal period.

The second method of measuring neuropils is by tedious microscopic counting, using in particular electron microscopy. As sections of cells are viewed only in part, and counts must usually be related to other subparts due to variations in size, section and exact location, errors in estimates of the various subparts are inevitable. Recent descriptions of Golgi stains of dendritic spines have shown alterations in retarded children[32–34] which are most likely nonspecific, but which could be due to a common cause such as disuse, undernutrition, seizures or anoxia. Similar studies have not been done in children with primary undernutrition, but would be of interest.

EFFECTS OF INTRAUTERINE UNDERNUTRITION

Estimates of neuropils by total ganglioside (NANA) determinations in brains of SGA and AGA infants have only been reported from our laboratory to date[8]. Neither the concentrations, expressed per mg wet weight, or per mg DNA, or the total brain ganglioside levels varied between the SGA and AGA brains. This suggests quantitative differences were not present in axon–dendritic terminations as a result of intrauterine undernutrition. Studies reporting histological neuropil data are not available to my knowledge.

EFFECTS OF POSTNATAL UNDERNUTRITION

Total quantities of brain gangliosides, used as an estimate of intact neuropils, have been measured in brains of infants dying with undernutrition between ages 1 and 2 years[15]. Statistically significant differences were not found in either concentration (per g wet weight or per mg DNA) or in total quantities between the undernourished and control infants. This was also true when results for total cerebrum–brain stem gangliosides were expressed for age-matched pairs, although the controls were consistently slightly higher. Concentrations were also measured in dissected white matter in the report of Fishman *et al.*[23]. Both the 4-month- and 12-month-old age-matched pairs had higher concentrations in the white matter from the undernourished infant.

I am unaware of light or electron microscopic studies evaluating neuropil intactness in children dying of undernutrition. Studies in undernourished rats have suggested some differences[35, 36] which may or may not apply to the human. Electroencephalogram studies of undernourished and rehabilitated infants have been reported to be abnormal in studies from our laboratory, including the cortical evoked response, as well as studies from numerous other laboratories as reviewed by Coursin[37]. The EEG is a gross physiological measurement depending on the intactness of many brain components, of which dendritic–axonal connections are only one.

GLYCOSAMINOGLYCANS

NORMAL DEVELOPMENT

As with most other brain biochemical components, the physiological significance of glycosaminoglycans (mucopolysaccharides) in the central nervous system has not been clearly defined. These polysaccharide–protein complexes include: hyaluronic acid, chondroitin sulphate, heparan sulphate, dermatan sulphate, heparin sulphate and others less well characterized. Several studies have suggested that these compounds play a role during myelination and during other maturation processes in brain[38-40]. The brain has a higher content of glycosaminoglycans than other organs such as liver, kidney and spleen[41], although the collagen content of brain is low and they are apparently not associated with collagen. Their polyuronic nature has led to speculation[42] that they may function in relation to cation and water exchange in maintenance of the blood/brain barrier, or possibly in nerve conduction. They are covalently linked to proteins and may also play a role in producing the structural rigidity of the brain. Their possible importance in relation to intelligence is suggested by brain glycosaminoglycan alterations which have been described with inherited mucopolysaccharide disorders associated with mental retardation[43].

As with brain protein, the glycosaminoglycans continue to be formed throughout life. Absolute quantities of total glycosaminoglycan per brain increase primarily before birth, but also show a twofold (Figure 2.2) postnatal increase to reach the adult quantity in the year following birth. The concentrations of brain glycosaminoglycans reach a peak in the newborn human brain, when they are twice as high as in the fetus or adult[44]. The major glycosaminoglycans found in newborn brain are hyaluronic acid, chondroitin sulphate and heparan sulphate. Levels of chondroitin sulphate are higher in the mature brain, whereas levels of heparan sulphate and hyaluronic acid are lower in adult brain[44]. Thus, changes in brain glycosaminoglycans with age are primarily in the dominant types of glycosaminoglycans present rather than in total quantities.

EFFECTS OF INTRAUTERINE UNDERNUTRITION

Glycosaminoglycans have been measured in brains from three SGA infants and three AGA infants[45]. The major alterations in the quantities of glycosaminoglycans in the SGA compared with the AGA brains were: (1) a decrease in the concentration of hyaluronic acid in the SGA brains (reduced 55% in brain purification fraction IA where most hyaluronic acid is located), (2) a reduction in chondroitin sulphate in the SGA brains (reduced 32% in purification fraction IIA where almost all chondroitin sulphate is found), (3) a reduction in heparan sulphate concentrations in the SGA brains (reduced 35 and 37% in purification fractions IB and IIA respectively, where heparan sulphate is primarily located). The concentrations of the low sulphated chondroitin sulphate and of the hyaluronidase-resistant galactosamine fractions were increased in the SGA brains. Hyaluronic acid formed 42% and 31% of the total glycosaminoglycans in the AGA and SGA brains respectively, whereas chondroitin sulphate formed 22 and 21% respectively. In both AGA and SGA brains heparan sulphate formed 26% of the total, whereas in adult brains heparan sulphate makes up only 6% of the total[44]. Low sulphated chondroitin sulphate made up 10% of the total in SGA brains, and 4% in the AGA brains. Unidentified galactosamine-containing compounds made up the other 12% in SGA brains, and the other 6% in AGA brains.

The formation of sulphated glycosaminoglycans (which include all compounds except hyaluronic acid) shares the same brain sulphation system (phosphoadenosine phosphosulphate) with sulphatide formation. As activity of the sulphation enzyme, galacto-cerebroside sulpho-transferase, was found reduced in the brains of SGA infants[9] and quantities and concentrations of sulphatide were also lower, it is not surprising that alterations were also found in the glycosaminoglycans following intrauterine deprivation. The implications and importance of these alterations are unknown at present.

EFFECTS OF POSTNATAL UNDERNUTRITION

Brain specimens from two children, ages 1 and 4 years, dying with postnatal undernutrition (kwashiorkor) have been analysed for glyco-saminoglycans[46]. Total glycosaminoglycan concentrations were reduced in both children in comparison with controls; values of 0.91 mg and 0.53 mg uronic acid/g dry defatted brain were obtained for the 1- and 4-year-old respectively, whereas a 1-year-old normal child had a value of 2.62 mg uronic acid/g. Hyaluronic acid was found to form 73% and 36% of the total glycosaminoglycans in the brain of the 1-year-old child with kwashiorkor and the 1-year-old control, respectively. Thus the differences were both qualitative and quantitative. It has not yet been ruled out that increased catabolism of glycosaminoglycans might not be occurring in these patients, as is suggested by the increased glyco-saminoglycan levels found in the urine of patients with postnatal undernutrition[47].

SUMMARY

Biochemical analyses of brains from human infants suffering from intrauterine or postnatal undernutrition have demonstrated alterations in quantities of brain cells, myelin lipid, brain protein and brain glyco-saminoglycans. The degree of reduction of any of these components is related to the timing of the undernutrition and is likely also related to the severity of the undernutrition. Results tend to be somewhat variable, but this is to be expected from human studies. Certainly the timing, severity, complicating illnesses, complicating vitamin deficiencies and the many other variables such as those illustrated in Figure 2.1 make the human infant a poor 'experimental model'. However, the fact that alterations in brain biochemistry do occur as a result of enviro-nutritional deprivation cannot be denied.

Further studies are needed in the areas of dendritic–axonal con-nections and neurotransmitters. In addition, there is a void in informa-tion concerning the effects of rehabilitation on the human brain. Analyses have not been performed on brains from low birth weight infants who had a period of normal growth after birth, and have not been performed on previously postnatally undernourished infants who underwent rehabilitation. Until such analyses are done, the permanence of the biochemical alterations described in the present studies can only be speculated on, using findings from laboratory animal studies. Certainly adequate environutritional stimulation for all of the world's infants would seem a major world priority in developing optimal adult potential.

ACKNOWLEDGEMENT

This work has been supported by Grant No. HS 0315-01AT0376A11111, NIH Retardation Studies, National Institutes of Health, Bethesda, Maryland.

REFERENCES

1. Mata, L. J. (1974). The relationship of maternal infection to fetal growth. In *Early Malnutrition and Mental Development*, p. 43 (J. Cravioto, L. Hambraeus and B. Vahlquist, editors) (Uppsala, Sweden: Almqvist and Wiksell)
2. Graham, G. G. and Blizzard, R. M. (1973). Thyroid hormonal studies in severely malnourished Peruvian infants and small children. In *Endocrine Aspects of Malnutrition*, p. 205 (L. I. Gardner and P. Amacher, editors) (Santa Ynez, California: The Kroc Foundation)
3. Chase, H. P. and Martin, H. P. (1970). Undernutrition and child development. *N. Engl. J. Med.*, **282**, 933
4. Nellhaus, G. (1968). Head circumference from birth to eighteen years: practical composite international and interracial graphs. *Pediatrics*, **41**, 106
5. Dobbing, J. and Sands, J. (1973). Quantitative growth and development of human brain. *Arch. Dis. Childh.*, **48**, 757
6. Chase, H. P., Dabiere, C. S., Welch, N. N. and O'Brien, D. (1971). Intrauterine undernutrition and brain development. *Pediatrics*, **47**, 491
7. Winick, M. (1968). Changes in nucleic acid and protein content of the human brain during growth. *Pediatr. Res.*, **2**, 352
8. Chase, H. P. (1973). The effects of intrauterine and postnatal undernutrition on normal brain development. *Ann. N.Y. Acad. Sci.*, **205**, 231
9. Chase, H. P., Welch, N. N., Dabiere, C. S., Vasan, N. S. and Butterfield, L. J. (1972). Alterations in human brain biochemistry following intrauterine growth retardation. *Pediatrics*, **50**, 403
10. Sarma, M. K. J. and Rao, K. S. (1974). Biochemical composition of different regions in brains of small for date infants. *J. Neurochem.*, **22**, 671
11. Lubchenco, L. O., Horner, F. A., Reed, L. H., Hix, I. E., Jr., Metcalf, D., Cohig, R., Elliott, H. C. and Bourg, M. (1963). Sequelae of premature birth. *Am. J. Dis. Child.*, **106**, 101
12. Chase, H. P., Dabiere, C. S., Welch, N. N. and O'Brien, D. (1971). Intrauterine undernutrition and brain development. *Pediatrics*, **47**, 491
13. Winick, M. and Rosso, P. (1969). The effect of severe early malnutrition on cellular growth of human brain. *Pediatr. Res.*, **3**, 181
14. Winick, M., Rosso, P. and Waterlow, J. (1970). Cellular growth of cerebrum, cerebellum, and brain stem in normal and marasmic children. *Exp. Neurol.*, **26**, 393
15. Chase, H. P., Canosa, C. A., Dabiere, C. S., Welch, N. N. and O'Brien,

D. (1974). Postnatal undernutrition and human brain development. *J. Ment. Def. Res.*, **18**, 355

16. Fish, I. and Winick, M. (1969). Effect of malnutrition on regional growth of the developing rat brain. *Exp. Neurol.*, **25**, 534

17. Chase, H. P., Lindsley, W. F. B., Jr. and O'Brien, D. (1969). Undernutrition and cerebellar development. *Nature (London)*, **221**, 554

18. Dow, R. S. (1970). Historical review of cerebellar investigation. In *The Cerebellum in Health and Disease*, (W. S. Fields and W. D. Willis, editors) p. 5 (St. Louis, Mo.: Warren H. Green, Inc)

19. Kritchevsky, D. and Holmes, W. L. (1962). Occurrence of desmosterol in developing rat brain. *Biochem. Biophys. Res. Commun.*, **7**, 128

20. Chase, H. P., Dorsey, J. and McKhann, G. (1967). The effect of malnutrition on the synthesis of a myelin lipid. *Pediatrics*, **40**, 551

21. Ghittoni, N. E. and Faryna de Raveglia, I. (1973). Effects of malnutrition and subsequent rehabilitation on the lipid composition of cerebral cortex and cerebellum of the rat. *J. Neurochem.*, **21**, 983

22. Graham, G. G. (1967). Effect of infantile malnutrition on growth. *Fed. Proc.*, **26**, 139

23. Fishman, M. A., Prensky, A. L. and Dodge, P. R. (1969). Low content of cerebral lipids in infants suffering from malnutrition. *Nature (London)*, **221**, 552

24. Rosso, P., Hormanzabal, J. and Winick, M. (1970). Changes in brain weight, cholesterol, phospholipid and DNA content in marasmic children. *Am. J. Clin. Nutr.*, **23**, 1275

25. Dobbing, J. (1963). The influence of early nutrition on the development and myelination of the brain. *Proc. R. Soc.*, **159**, 503

26. Barkel, A., Mahudik, S. and Rapport, M. D. (1974). Flow in vivo of glucose carbon to brain protein in rats: effect of starvation. *J. Neurochem.*, **22**, 511

27. Hyden, H. and Egyhozi, E. (1964). Changes in RNA content and base composition in cortical neurons of rats in a learning experiment involving transfer of handedness. *Proc. Nat. Acad. Sci.*, **52**, 1030

28. Hess, H. H. and Thalheimer, C. (1965). Microassay of biochemical structural components in nervous tissues. I. Extraction and partition of lipids and assay of nucleic acids. *J. Neurochem.*, **12**, 193

29. Economo, C. V. (1927). *Zellaufbau der grosshirnrinde des Mensched* (Berlin: Springer-Verlag)

30. Bass, N. H., Netsky, M. G. and Young, E. (1970). Effect of neonatal malnutrition on developing cerebrum. I. Microchemical and histological study of cellular differentiation in the rat. *Arch. Neurol.*, **23**, 289

31. Svennerholm, L. (1974). Lipid biochemical changes of brain during development. In *Early Malnutrition and Mental Development* (J. Cravioto, L. Hambraeus and B. Vahlquist, editors) p. 67 (Uppsala, Sweden: Almqvist and Wiksell)

32. Marin-Padilla, M. (1972). Structural abnormalities of the cerebral cortex

in human chromosomal aberrations: a Golgi study. *Brain Res.*, **44**, 625

33. Purpura, D. P. (1974). Dendritic spine 'dysgenesis' and mental retardation. *Science*, **186**, 1126

34. Huttenlocher, P. (1974). Dendritic development in neocortex of children with mental defect and infantile spasms. *Neurology*, **24**, 203

35. Neville, H. E. and Chase, H. P. (1971). Undernutrition and cerebellar development. *Exp. Neurol.*, **33**, 485

36. Cragg, B. G. (1972). The development of cortical synapses during starvation in the rat. *Brain*, **95**, 143

37. Coursin, D. B. (1974). Electrophysiologic studies in malnutrition. In *Early Malnutrition and Mental Development*, (J. Cravioto, L. Hambraeus and B. Vahlquist editors) p. 72 (Uppsala, Sweden: Almqvist and Wiksell)

38. Brante, G. (1959). Mucopolysaccharides and mucoids of the nervous system. In *Biochemistry of the Central Nervous System*, (F. Brucke, editor) p. 291 (New York: Pergamon Press)

39. Singh, M. and Bachhawat, B. K. (1965). The distribution and variation with age of different uronic acid-containing mucopolysaccharides in brain. *J. Neurochem.*, **12**, 519

40. Szabo, M. M. and Roboz-Einstein, E. (1962). Acidic polysaccharides in the central nervous system. *Arch. Biochem. Biophys.*, **98**, 406

41. Margolis, R. U. (1967). Acid mucopolysaccharides and proteins of bovine whole brain, white matter and myelin. *Biochim. Biophys. Acta*, **141**, 91

42. Chandrasekharan, E. V. and Bachhawat, B. K. (1969). Effect of carrageenin and cortisone on the formation of cultivated connective tissue. I. Isolation and characterisation of glycosaminoglycans. *Biochim. Biophys. Acta*, **177**, 265

43. Constantopoulos, G. and DeKaban, A. S. (1971). Content and distribution of molecular weights of mucopolysaccharides in the brain and other organs of Hurler's patients. *J. Neuropathol. Exp. Neurol.*, **30**, 144

44. Singh, M. and Bachhawat, B. K. (1968). Isolation and characterization of glycosaminoglycans in human brain of different age groups. *J. Neurochem.*, **15**, 249

45. Vasan, N. S. and Chase, H. P. (1975). Brain glycosaminoglycans (mucopolysaccharides) following intrauterine growth retardation. *Biol. Neonate*. (In press)

46. Chandrasekaran, E. V., Mukherjee, K. L. and Bachhawat, B. K. (1971). Isolation and characterization of glycosaminoglycans from brain of children with protein-calorie malnutrition. *J. Neurochem.*, **18**, 1913

47. Cherian, R., Chandrasekaran, E. V. and Bachhawat, B. K. (1970): Glycosaminoglycans of human urine: Part III. Isolation and characterisation of urinary glycosaminoglycans in normal and kwashiorkor children. *Indian J. Biochem.*, **7**, 174

CHAPTER 3

Prenatal nutrition and mental competence

Z. A. STEIN AND M. W. SUSSER

INTRODUCTION

Poor mental performance, social deprivation and nutritional deprivation
are commonly found in the same strata of society, and in the same social
situations. Over the past two decades, it came to be realized that poor
nutrition, in particular malnutrition in prenatal and early postnatal life,
could be a major factor in the social distribution of depressed mental
competence[1, 2]. No one will dispute the importance of mental competence, for societies as well as individuals, in coping with the modern
world. If nutrition in early prenatal or postnatal life is a cause of
depressed mental competence, the social implications are immense.
Although malnutrition is eminently preventable, not only by the production of more food, but by its equitable distribution and by its
educated use, it remains widespread in the world.

The broad hypothesis generated by these circumstances and related
scientific work is that early malnutrition, including prenatal malnutrition, retards brain growth, and that the brain's organic deficit in turn
leads to mental deficits[3]. The probable population-wide manifestations
of the effects of malnutrition on mental performance would be depressed
IQ, and a raised prevalence of the so-called cultural–familial syndrome
of mild mental retardation[4]. In this syndrome, which affects about 3%
of the population in their teens, the mental retardation is unaccom-
panied by detectable signs of organic impairment, and as with depressed
IQ, the condition is virtually confined to the poorest and the most
deprived sections of the population[5–9]. Thus it has the same distribution
as nutritional deprivation. Brain damage, and severe mental retardation
accompanied by detectable organic lesions, do not display the same
dramatic social gradient as mild mental retardation. Thus severe

mental retardation has a distribution that diverges from that of nutritional deprivation, and one would not anticipate finding it among the consequences of early malnutrition.

Speculation about the effect of nutrition on human intelligence is plentiful and knowledge scant. Little evidence bears directly on the relationship. In humans, the evidence is drawn from observational studies of the association of early nutritional deprivation either with retarded brain growth at autopsy, or with retarded mental development in later childhood. Other evidence is drawn, by analogy, from animal experiments. These experiments likewise test the effects of early nutritional deprivation either on brain growth or on subsequent mental development, but none complete the sequence.

Human studies relating to the sequence of nutritional deprivation, retarded brain growth or fetal growth, and subsequent mental development will be the subject of the present chapter. Several studies concerned with nutrition and brain or fetal growth will be discussed in the section that follows. In order to examine the full sequence of prenatal nutritional experience through adult mental competence, we must rely on the study of the Dutch famine, which alone so far provides data on all three components in the hypothetical sequence.

PRENATAL GROWTH AS A POTENTIALLY CRITICAL PHASE OF DEVELOPMENT

The phase of development of an organism is thought to moderate the effects of exposure to an insult. The period of most active growth of the brain is supposedly its critical period, the time of its greatest vulnerability to insult and irreversible damage. With regard to nutritional deprivation, a number of experiments on rats, dogs and pigs support the critical period postulate. In rats, nutritional deprivation at the time of maximum brain growth reduced the estimated number of brain cells, and the number remained deficient thereafter[10, 11]. Myelin deposition also was found to be restricted and to remain deficient in studies of dogs and pigs[12, 13]. At least a part of the phase of maximum growth in the human brain takes place in the prenatal period. In consequence, the prenatal period has been a focus of research because of its potential significance as a critical developmental phase with regard to nutritional insults in particular.

Some of the apparent inconsistencies in critical period experiments can be accounted for by the fact that species vary in the phase of life at which the maximum rate of brain growth takes place[14, 15]. In pigs, for instance, the peak growth rate is prenatal, while in rats it is postnatal. If birth is seen as an event that supervenes earlier or later in embryonic development among different species, we can explain the vulnerability of the brain of the rat (born at an early stage of development) to experimental nutritional deficiency in the immediate postnatal phase, and of the brain of the pig (born at a later stage of development) in the prenatal phase.

The critical period hypothesis is not supported in every respect by experiments on growth. In some experiments, no effects from starvation during the maximum growth period could be demonstrated; the investigators found a raised ratio of brain weight to body weight which they believed indicated a relative sparing of the brain[16]. McCance and Widdowson[15], comparing growth rates in different species undernourished at various ages, considered that a critical period of development might occur when, early in life, 'the regulating centres of the hypothalamus are being co-ordinated with . . . rate of growth'. The runt in a pig litter, born underweight, is presumed to be deprived of nutrients *in utero* by deficient blood supply. If the runt is well-fed after birth, it grows at the normal rate for its size and age, stops growing at the same age as its littermates, becomes a normally formed adult, but remains small. Thus, although the pattern of growth is normal, the gap induced by the presumed prenatal disturbance of the hypothalamus is never made up. Prenatal determination of growth pattern lends support to the notion of a critical period.

On the other hand, McCance and Widdowson did not fully reconcile their findings with the notion of a single critical period, determined by the brain growth spurt. They produced malformed organs in pigs by postnatal and not by prenatal protein malnutrition. In pigs of normal birth weight, severe malnutrition after birth greatly slowed growth. When rehabilitated, such pigs showed rapid 'catch-up' growth, and also continued to grow beyond the age when littermates had ceased growing. The investigators believe that postnatal malnutrition temporarily disturbed a growth pattern that was set in prenatal life. With rehabilitation, the prenatally determined pattern reasserted itself, and adjustments in the rate and duration of growth brought the pigs close to their predetermined size. Unlike the runts, however, certain organs were malformed, presumably because of deficient diet at the growing period combined with selective access of the organs to the limited nutrient supply.

A theory that postulates a critical period of brain growth must take account of at least two recognized growth processes. One process, hyperplasia, refers to an increase in cell number; the other process, hypertrophy, refers to an increase in cell size. Hyperplasia of brain cells and hypertrophy of brain cells take place at separate phases of development. To complicate matters further, different anatomical structures and cell types of the brain have different timetables. Thus in the rat, the growth of the cortex, hindbrain and cerebellum proceeds each according to its own schedule[17].

Hyperplasia and hypertrophy of two cell types, neurones (the functional cells of the nervous system) and glia (the connective tissue cells of the nervous system) contribute asynchronously to rapid brain growth. In humans hyperplasia of neurons seems mainly to occur in the second trimester of pregnancy[18]. Maximum velocity of growth in total brain weight has been placed at a later phase, in the months just before and after birth. Both neurones and glia are thought to contribute to the rapid growth of these months. In this phase, the growth of neurones occurs in the form of hypertrophy, and the growth of glia in the form of hyperplasia. The hypertrophy of neurones continues with their arborization into dendrites and synapses. The recent work of Dobbing and Sands (1973)[19] shows this phase of rapid growth extending through the second year of life.

Nutritional deprivation in humans can seldom be pinpointed in time with the precision required by a test of the critical period hypothesis. No evidence bears on the effects of malnutrition during the postulated period of hyperplasia of neurones in the second trimester of gestation. Although some evidence relates to the effects of malnutrition during the postulated period of combined hyperplasia and hypertrophy of brain cells in late prenatal and infant life, the chains of inference are long. Thus the timing implied by observations from autopsy studies of brains of a few infants who died of acute malnutrition is compatible with a critical period effect produced by nutritional insult. Those who died during the first year of life had a marked deficiency of cell number in the brain, while those who died in the second year of life had no such deficiency. The finding suggests that malnutrition during gestation or in early infancy but not later had affected brain cell proliferation[20]. The deficiency of cell number was more marked in infants of low birth weight. Prenatal malnutrition is a plausible cause of such low birth weight, and hence of retarded brain growth in these infants[21].

Some recent interpretations have clouded the specificity of the critical period hypothesis. One question relates to the timing of the maximum growth of the two-cell types, and another to the duration of the maximum growth period. Both questions influence predictions about the effects of injury or deprivation sustained at different phases of growth.

The problem of timing arises from the asynchrony between the early phase of hyperplasia of neurones during the second trimester, and the later phase of hypertrophy of neurones and hyperplasia of glia during the third trimester and later. The appeal of the critical period hypothesis rests in part on the fact that neurones, unlike connective tissue cells, are irreplaceable (although their extensions may regenerate) and that the integrity of neurons underlies the integrity of brain function. On this basis the second trimester of pregnancy, when neurones multiply, seems more likely to be a critical period in which irreversible damage might occur than does the third trimester, when glia multiply and neurones grow larger and extend their dendrites. Thus while the third trimester is the prenatal phase of maximum brain growth, and also the period when fetal growth in general is most sensitive to nutritional deprivation, it may not be the period when the most critical brain development occurs. Moreover, during neuronal hyperplasia in the second trimester, the nutritional needs of the fetus may be small enough for the mother to sustain under any conditions that support her own life. Hence the fetus may be protected from irreversible damage to neurons.

The problem of the duration of the period of maximum brain growth may also detract from the importance of prenatal growth in the third trimester for subsequent development. The longer is the period of rapid growth, the longer is the duration of the period of deprivation required to produce irreversible brain impairment likely to be. Short periods of deprivation covering a small fraction of the critical period might be recoverable or undetectable. Since the most recent research indicates that rapid brain growth may persist into the second year of life or longer, prenatal deprivation alone might not be decisive if rapid brain growth continues for a long time postnatally. In fact, the later postnatal period might be critical for arborization of dendrites and establishing the connections between synapses. [18]

NUTRITION AND FETAL GROWTH

A review of this aspect of the hypothetical causal sequence leading to diminished mental competence at once meets problems in measuring both nutrient intake and fetal growth including brain growth. With regard to the seemingly simple technical problem of measuring nutrient intake, an adequate test of the hypothesis requires an adequate measure of nutrient intake for sufficient numbers over a sufficient period of time. No means of making valid measurements of nutrient intake in large numbers in a population of free-living human beings are ordinarily available. The absence of precise measures of intake leads to difficulties in interpretation of all observation studies made under the circumstances of everyday living. Rapid and dramatic changes in dietary intake, such as happens with war or famine, may afford opportunities to overcome this type of difficulty. The necessary data on available nutrients and dietary adaptations, and the vital statistics which enable the exposed population to be defined, are seldom available in the conditions of crisis and disaster.

The difficulty can be circumvented, although partially at best, by experimental intervention. A number of attempts to carry out such experiments by giving measured food supplements to pregnant women living in poor circumstances and presumed to have poor diets have been carried out. Even so, there is no direct means of assuring that food supplements do not serve as substitutes for regular diet, so long as there is no good measure of regular diet. Resort must be made to such indirect means as monitoring maternal weight. In the discussion that follows, we shall subdivide the material according to whether the study was observational and related to everyday living, or whether it was observational and related to war and famine, and third, whether it involved experimental intervention.

With regard to measuring the impact of prenatal nutrition on fetal growth, histopathological and biochemical measures of brain cell growth have been developed and applied, but the application of such measures in relation to nutritionally deprived fetuses has been by necessity exceptionally rare. Dobbing and Sands have reported on a substantial series of autopsies among infants who died of causes unrelated to nutrition[19] while Winick and co-workers[22, 23] have reported on four cases of malnourished infants who were also of low birth weight and nine others of normal birth weight.

In all substantial series in which some measure of nutritional deprivation can be related to some measure of fetal outcome, however, the index of effect has been much more indirect. Among fetal dimensions, birth weight is the one most frequently and reliably measured, but of course its correlation with brain growth is by no means complete. Head size may perhaps reflect brain growth more closely than do other fetal dimensions[24], but it has been less frequently measured than birth weight. A third type of index that is available and can be related to prenatal nutritional intake is prenatal and infant mortality. Mortality, the obverse of survival, perhaps provides an indicator of infant vital functions including cerebral functions. Certainly fetal growth, and particularly birth weight, has been shown to bear a close relationship to perinatal mortality and survival[21, 25–27].

EVERYDAY DIET AND FETAL GROWTH

Many attempts have been made to discover associations between everyday diet and the outcome of pregnancy. The results are not consistent, and detailed analysis seems called for to try and reconcile them.

Most of these studies suffer from one or more problems of design and execution. In short they have had small numbers, inappropriate controls, and probable selection bias. They sometimes failed to ensure that histories were obtained and recorded independent of knowledge of the outcome; all suffered from the notorious difficulties of obtaining accurate long-term diet histories or of extrapolating from short-term histories. In some instances investigators have taken current diet histories during pregnancy, although often late in its course. In other instances they have taken retrospective histories covering the entire pregnancy, and even the time before conception. In at least two case-control studies the diet histories were obtained after the birth of the infants, without any reported control of the possible bias of the interviewers due to their knowledge of outcome.

Two of these several diet surveys deserve detailed consideration, both because they took care to control some of these sources of error, and because they were the main force in the swing of fashion against the nutritional hypothesis as an explanation of low birth weight. A study in Nashville from 1945 to 1949 included all the 2300 pregnant women admitted to the prenatal clinic at Vanderbilt University Hospital[28, 29]. Their nutritional state was established by clinical examination, bio-chemical studies, and diet histories at more than one period of gestation, and the obstetrician was blind to the appraisals of nutrition. Low birth weight infants comprised 5.6% among 2046 deliveries. The mothers of low birth weight infants were found to have had a lower intake and blood level of vitamin C, and on physical examination they were more often found to be 'undernourished'. There was no association of other dietary items and biochemical findings with low birth weight.

This careful dietary history study shares with others difficulties in validating both dietary histories and appraisals of nutritional state made by many clinical observers. Another question is raised by the social selection evident in the sample. The hospital set minimum and maximum incomes for eligibility. At the outset there were paying and free patients, but midway through the study minimal charges for all were levied for outpatient visits and hospital delivery. All the women were white; 95% were married and 67% enrolled for care during the first or second trimester. The low birth weight rate of 5.6% confirmed that these women were not a group at high risk. The influence of food intake on prematurity is unlikely to be perceived where the room for variation is small.

The room for variation of birth weight with nutrition could have been further reduced by the counselling and care the women received. Vitamin or mineral supplements were given to the women most in need. More than a quarter (27%) of the sample received these supplements, so that dietary disparities were likely to have been diminished. These supplements were not included in calculating nutrient intakes; thus differences in diet between women may have been recorded where there were none, and effects of these differences sought where there could be none.

A well-controlled dietary survey was carried out in Aberdeen in the North of Scotland by A. M. Thomson[30]. Thomson rejected the simple diet history method, for he found that it failed to give valid information in the Aberdeen population. He used mothers' reports of weighed intake of food over a single week, measured against the observations of dieticians. These reports proved to be more valid than diet histories, and they were reasonably reliable when repeated.

Thomson collected reports of weighed food intake during 1 week from 713 primigravida in the seventh month of pregnancy. Only 489 (68.5%) 'reliable' records were analysed. The attributes of the women included were biased toward less prematurity. Most results were reported only in terms of calories, because of the high correlation between calories and other nutrients.

Reported caloric intake was considerably less among women of the lower than of the upper social classes[31]. It was also less among short than among tall women, and this relationship held whether the mother was underweight, of average weight, or overweight. Finally, with regard to the variable of central concern, caloric intake was less among women who had babies of low birth weight. The correlation virtually disappeared, however, when maternal body weight was held constant. The actual correlation was then reduced to $r = 0.05$. On the other hand, when caloric intake was held constant, the correlation between maternal body weight and birth weight persisted ($r = 0.29$). Thomson therefore discounted the correlation between calories and birth weight as spurious; he considered that it was 'explained' by the correlation of an antecedent factor, 'maternal body size', with both caloric intake and birth weight[30, 32].

Thomson's negative conclusion cannot be accepted without reserve. Two specific points of difficulty can be recognized. First, it is a large assumption that the food a woman reports she has weighed in one week during the seventh month of pregnancy fairly represents the whole 40 weeks of pregnancy, although Thomson did provide evidence to show that reported dietary intake varied less among individual pregnant women during pregnancy than between women at the same stage of pregnancy. Second, Thomson calculated maternal size from the weights of women recorded at 20 weeks of pregnancy. A great part of the weight gain in pregnancy (apart from the products of conception and water retention, as Thomson and co-workers themselves have demonstrated) takes place between the tenth and thirtieth weeks of pregnancy and is stored as fat[33, 34] One study has found that the association of birth weight with maternal weight gain was related to early pregnancy in particular[35]. Thus weight at 20 weeks is influenced by much of the weight gain of the current pregnancy. This weight, taken as an index of 'maternal size', is therefore a variable which could be the result of caloric intake during pregnancy, when it would occur as an intervening variable between caloric intake and birth weight. Studies reported below clarify this point to some degree.

THOMSON'S HYPOTHESIS:

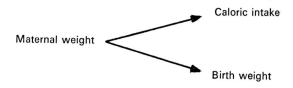

Alternate hypothesis:

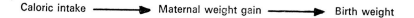

WAR, FAMINE AND FETAL GROWTH

Several studies have been made in unusual wartime conditions. The siege of Leningrad lasted 18 months, from August 1941 to January 1943, and conditions were of extreme severity for the 6 months from September 1941 until February 1942[36]. Food allowances were small in quantity and of low nutritional value. The diet consisted mainly of bread, one-half of it made up of defective rye flour and the rest of such substitutes as cellulose, malt and bran. Many thousands died of starvation.

During the early part of the siege, in the latter half of 1941, a significant decrease in average weight at birth was noted[37]. During the first half of 1942 the average birth weight of babies carried to term was 529 g less for boys, and 542 g less for girls, than it was during the last half of 1941. Forty-nine per cent of those born in the first half of 1942 weighed less than 2500 g.

During the siege the women experienced severe strains in addition to deficient diet. They suffered from excessive physical exertion, lack of rest, constant nervous tension and cold. The possible contribution of these factors to low birth weight cannot be assessed.

World War II provided a second study relevant to nutrition in pregnancy. Births recorded in Wuppertal, Germany, for the period 1937–1948 revealed a slight decrease in mean birth weights in 1940[38]. The birth weights then remained steady until 1945, when there was an abrupt fall to a level 185 g below that of 1937–1939. After the abrupt fall in mean birth weights in that year, there followed a steady rise, until in 1948 the prewar level of 1937–1939 was reached.

In Germany the year 1945 was one of chaotic living conditions and acute food shortage. The official ration for pregnant women at that time supposedly provided sufficient calories, but in practice full rations seemed never to be available, and the special rations that pregnant and lactating women did receive were commonly shared with members of the family. Pregnant women were somewhat below the weights usual in more normal times. In these before and after comparisons, uncontrolled historical factors accompanying the food shortage cannot be ruled out as contributory causes of low birth weight.

Further support for the nutritional hypothesis can be found in the effects of the wartime famine in western Holland during the winter of 1944–1945. The effects of the famine can be defined better in the Dutch than in the Leningrad experience, because in Holland the famine period was sharply demarcated and accompanied by fewer and less severe privations of other kinds. Overwork and other strains were not of the same order as in Leningrad, and there was probably less fetal damage and loss.

In a study of clinic records, C. A. Smith showed that during the famine there was a downward shift in the distribution of mean birth weights[39]. Birth weights declined to a nadir after about 18 to 21 weeks of famine, and began to rise again immediately after the famine ended. As Smith pointed out, the fact that the mean birth weight neither declined continuously throughout the famine nor continued low after the famine is of special interest, because it supports the notion that the fall in mean birth weight reflected nutrition in late pregnancy.

Our own studies confirm and extend these results of Smith[40-42]. The famine in Holland was extremely well circumscribed in place and time, being confined to large cities of the West, Amsterdam, Rotterdam, Leiden and others. It was the result of a transport embargo imposed by the Nazi occupation on West Holland in reprisal for a strike of Dutch rail workers in aid of the Allied forces trying to cross the Rhine[43]

(Figure 3.1). It lasted almost exactly 6 months, from October 1944 to the first week in May 1945 when the Allied forces finally crossed the Rhine. We used these circumstances of place and time in our design.

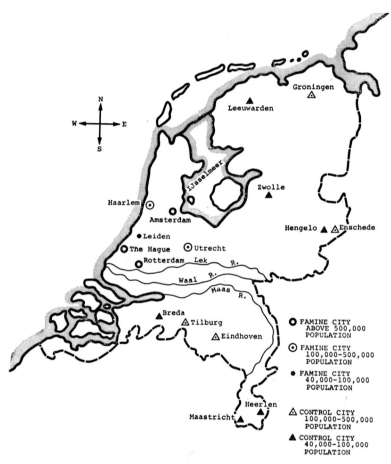

Figure 3.1   The Netherlands. (Taken from Stein, Z., Susser, M., Saenger, G. and Marolla, F. (1975) [40])

We compared infants born in the famine area with those born outside the famine area. Also, in order to test the critical period hypothesis, we selected births according to the particular period of exposure during gestation. In Figure 3.2, the retrospective cohort design used in our study is illustrated. Along the horizontal a time scale is shown. Each bar represents a one-month cohort of births. The bars labelled 'A' represent cohorts which were not exposed to famine in the prenatal period, but were exposed in the postnatal period. The bars labelled 'B' and 'C' were exposed to the famine late in the pregnancy and were born at the height of the famine. The cohort labelled 'D' were exposed early in pregnancy and born after the famine, while the cohorts labelled 'E' had no prenatal exposure to famine at all.

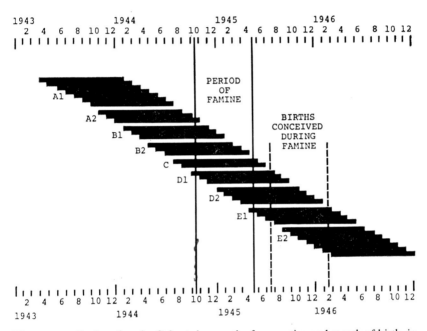

Figure 3.2 Design of study. Cohorts by month of conception and month of birth, in the Netherlands, 1943 through 1946, related to famine exposure. Solid vertical lines bracket the period of famine, and broken vertical lines bracket the period of births conceived during famine. (Taken from Stein, Z., Susser, M., Saenger, G. and Marolla, F. (1975) [40])

Using these facts of place and time of birth, we were able to examine the effects of the famine on infant growth in several dimensions. With regard to birth weight, food deprivation affected birth weight only in the third trimester (Figure 3.3). The effect was to shift birth weight fairly evenly to the left of the weight range. The effect of food intake during the third trimester on birth weight is not linear. Below the threshold value of caloric rations chosen to demonstrate the famine condition (1500 calories daily average in the third trimester) there was a significant effect of food rations on birth weight; above the threshold, there was none. With first trimester exposure, excess of very low birth weight infants was present among those conceived at the height of the famine—the cohort labelled 'D2' on the diagram and exposed early in gestation. The result is not statistically significant.

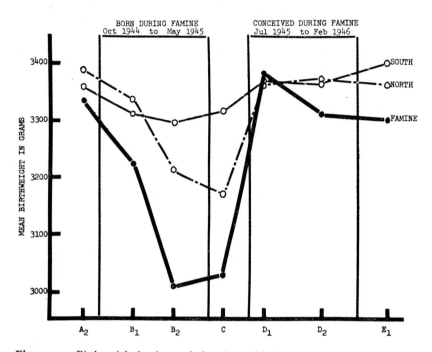

Figure 3.3 Birth weight by time and place (mean birth weight in grams for consecutive births in maternity hospitals for seven birth cohorts: famine, Northern control, and Southern control areas compared for the period August 1944 to March 1946 inclusive). (Taken from Stein, Z., Susser, M., Saenger, G. and Marolla, F. (1975) [40])

An effect of prenatal nutrition on infant length at birth was also present, although slight compared with that on birth weight (Figure 3.4). As with birth weight, the effect was both non-linear and confined to exposure to famine during the third trimester.

The results for head size (Figure 3.5) show essentially the same pattern as those for birth weight and for length. The effects of nutritional deprivation on head circumference were related to third trimester prenatal famine exposure and were non-linear. The result in relation to head

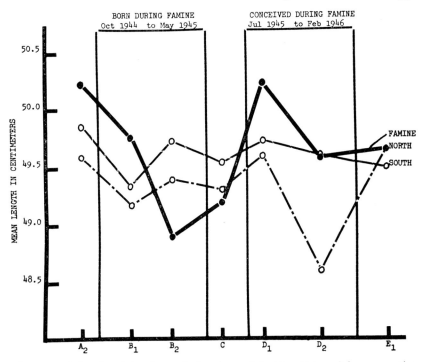

Figure 3.4 Infant length by time and place (mean infant length in cm) for consecutive births in maternity hospitals for seven birth cohorts: famine, Northern control, and Southern control areas compared for the period August 1944 to March 1946 inclusive). (Taken from Stein, Z., Susser, M., Saenger, G. and Marolla, F. (1975) [40])

size is of particular importance to the question under discussion as head size has been invested with biological significance as an index of brain growth and later development. Head size has been shown to be smaller in malnourished children than in comparison groups[40-42]. In such children, small head size occurs conjointly with other small body measurements, particularly height and weight. Small head size also seem to accompany retarded fetal growth[47-51]. Conversely, an increased rate of growth in head size in premature infants after birth has been attributed to improved nutrition brought about by changed hospital feeding practices[52]. In premature infants born at Hammersmith Hospital in London in 1965–1968, head size increased more rapidly than in cohorts born 4 years earlier.

Thus head size varies with growth and nutrition. Other studies indicate that head size is linked with brain size, and that brain size may

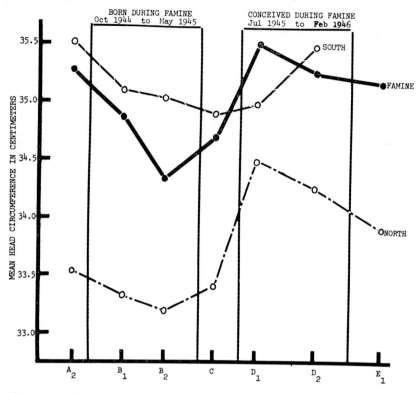

Figure 3.5 Head circumference of infants by time and place (mean head circumference of infants in centimeters for consecutive births in maternity hospitals for seven birth cohorts: famine, Northern control, and Southern control areas compared for the period August 1944 to March 1946 inclusive). (Taken from Stein, Z., Susser, M., Saenger, G. and Marolla, F. (1975) [40])

be influenced by nutrition. In East African autopsy studies, the brains of malnourished children weighed less than others[53]. In a small number of children who died of malnutrition and were compared at autopsy with children who had no signs of malnutrition, small head size has been found to relate also to reduced cell number in the brain[17]. Other evidence points to an association between head size and mental function and behaviour[54, 55].

Finally, the data of the Dutch famine showed a clear effect of food rations on postpartum maternal weight. The effects were again confined to famine exposure in the third trimester of pregnancy. Unlike all other indices of the reproductive process, the effect of food intake on maternal weight was linear, and there was no evidence of a threshold above which the effect was absent. Maternal weight can be taken as an index of the severity of the famine. From maternal weight change it could be inferred also that maternal nutrient stores afforded a buffer against the effects of nutritional deprivation on the fetus until those stores were depleted.

In summary, it could be concluded that there was a threshold value of maternal nutrient intake around which the strength of nutritional effects changed. The growth of the bones that determined fetal length and head size were less affected by nutritional deprivation than the growth of other tissues that determined fetal weight, such as fat and muscle. These effects of famine on fetal growth were not mediated through the shortening of gestation. The data from the Dutch famine thus enable us to argue, at least under the special condition of nutritional deprivation, that caloric intake produced the changes in the outcomes of the reproductive process. Rations determined caloric intake, which can safely be considered an antecedent of the changes that accompanied it. This assumption is not as safe under non-famine conditions, when Thomson's inference that mother's size determined both her caloric intake and the baby's weight cannot be ruled out[30, 32].

The third measure of the effect of prenatal nutrition on fetal growth and development is that of vitality in the post-natal period. In the circumstances of the Dutch famine, we found that exposure to famine produced an excess of deaths in the first 3 months of life[40, 56]. Exposure during the first trimester produced an excess of stillbirths and first-week deaths; these were seemingly linked with an excess of premature deliveries since both occurred in the same cohorts. Exposure during the third trimester produced an excess of deaths from 7–90 days of age; these were seemingly linked with low birth weights since again both phenomena occurred in the same cohorts.

INTERVENTION STUDIES

We turn next to studies based on an experimental model. Their difficulties are also great, and some are similar to those of observational studies. For instance, the vagaries of patients in following dietary advice and using supplements, and the inaccuracies of diet histories, render knowledge of the experimental input uncertain. Non-compliance affects the comparability of treatments groups; the motivation to comply may be associated both with certain food habits, and with birth weight levels, and confound the association of treatment and birth weight. Again, it is difficult to achieve a double blind trial with equality of treatment between groups and observations of outcome uncontaminated by knowledge of the treatment. None the less, one can hope to attain better control of hidden and confounding variables than with observational studies.

Seven experimental studies, all therapeutic experiments that aimed to raise birth weights by supplying the nutrients thought to be deficient, deserve detailed attention.

Five thousand women attending antenatal clinics in the London area in 1938 to 1939 were assigned alternately to an experimental group supplemented with vitamins and minerals, and to a control group[57]. The supplement was decided upon after a preliminary diet history study of 1000 pregnant women using the same clinics. In the experimental group there was some indication of a decrease in prematurity by dates, but there was no increase in birth weight.

In Canada in 1941 Ebbs assigned women attending a prenatal clinic to three groups on the basis of dietary history[58]. One group of women taking poor diets was left as a control and given placebo capsules of corn oil. A second group on a poor diet was given, during the last 3 or 4 months of pregnancy, added supplies of food, vitamins and minerals together with diet advice. A third group, found to be on a moderately good diet, was given diet advice alone. During pregnancy the obstetrician rated the condition and progress of each patient unaware of her assigned group. 'Many' of the patients in the supplemented group were visited at home to check on the consumption of the food being sent. In addition, a worker visited the homes of a 'small number' of patients in each group and weighed the food after it had been estimated and recorded by the women.

At term the supplemented group had higher haemoglobin and ascorbic acid values and lower phosphate values than the other two groups, levels compatible with the content of the diet supplement. The percentage of premature births reported in the control group with poor diet was 8.0; in the group given a supplemented diet it was 2.2; and in the group on an unsupplemented good diet and given dietary advice it was 3.0.

The interpretation of the study is not straightforward. The term 'premature birth' is not defined in the report, but the average birth weights are given. These birth weights appear anomalous; they were 7 lb 10 oz, 7 lb 7 oz and 7 lb 6½ oz, respectively. The unsupplemented group numbered 120 and the supplemented group numbered 90 when there was supposed to have been alternate assignment to each group. The two groups selected for study because their diet was poor appear to have been comparable in average age, in the proportion of primipara, and in other social factors. But the past obstetric history of abortions, prematures and stillbirths, which are events associated with birth weight, reveal different frequencies among the three groups.

A Scottish study during World War II represents another version of an experiment in diet supplementation[59]. During the last 3 months of pregnancy 500 women attending prenatal clinics received special supervision. Alternate women served as controls. The supervision consisted of detailed diet counselling and 'it was seen to that they made application for their priority allowances of food'. This allowance included a significant amount of meat, fruit juice and vitamin D. There were 31 premature births in the treatment group and 50 among the controls. There is no indication of an attempt to determine whether the supplementary food was actually obtained and ingested by the women. The authors indicate that the results are significant but the reported data is not sufficient for critical evaluation.

At about the same time, a Chicago group supplemented diets of pregnant women with minerals in a proprietary cereal preparation, or vitamins, or a combination of both, but in this study no increase in birth weights was detected[60]. Greater weight gain by the mothers in the three treatment groups, as compared to the untreated control, was interpreted by the investigators as evidence that the supplements were used and did have some effect. This study attempted to control the possible diversion of the supplements to other members of the family by providing sufficient supplements for the entire family. An unexplained anomaly in the design is that the 4 comparison groups, said to be selected at random, varied in size from 98 to 179.

A fifth experiment with supplements was conducted in Philadelphia from 1947 to 1953[61]. Patients registering for prenatal care (excepting those seriously ill, or unmarried, or at a stage beyond 16 weeks gestation) were assigned 'seriatim' to four groups, kept equal in respect to colour, age and parity. One group received a protein concentrate as a supplement, a second group a polyvitamin capsule, a third group both the protein and vitamins, and a fourth group received neither. All groups were given the same diet instruction. Because of the exclusions from the study, the rate of low birth weight to be expected among the regular population of the same hospital was probably higher than the 12.8% found in their 'coloured' control group.

The differences between the four groups in the percentage of birth weights under 5.5 lb were not statistically significant. Significant differences appeared, however, when those marginal babies weighing 5.1 to 5.5 lb and with a history of 39 or more weeks of gestation were excluded from the premature category. With this refinement, the difference between the group supplemented with protein and vitamins and the controls was significant $(P < 0.05)$. The difference between the protein and vitamin supplement group and the 3 other groups combined was of borderline significance $(P = 0.05)$.

This study was flawed in that 'some' patients who would not or could not take the protein and/or vitamin supplement were reassigned. These patients were replaced in their original group by the next available matching case to enroll at the clinic. The mothers dropped from the protein and vitamin group were reassigned to the control group. These reassignments resulted in groups of unequal size.

The reassigned patients did not differ from others in their original groups by colour, age, parity, education or income. Yet the fact that their behaviour was different with regard to taking supplements makes it possible that they were different in attributes that influence birth weight. It took time and effort to mix the protein supplement with milk to obtain a palatable drink. Thus some women at high risk of producing infants of low birth weight might have been removed from the protein supplemented groups and added to the control and vitamin only groups.

A sixth intervention study was carried out in four rural villages in Guatemala[62]. Chronic malnutrition of mild to moderate degree characterized this population. In two of the villages, initially intended as controls, pregnant women were offered a fluid supplement containing calories in the form of sugar without protein; in the two other villages, pregnant women were offered a fluid supplement in which 17% of the calories came from protein. The supplements were dispensed at a centre in each village. Pregnant women were encouraged to attend and to drink as much as they wished. At each attendance the exact amount taken was carefully recorded. All families with pre-school children were visited fortnightly to check on the advent of pregnancy or of illness among the women. Birth weight was recorded to the nearest 20 g within 24 hours of birth.

Among 423 live births, 288 were singletons of known gestation (in that last menstrual period had been reliably determined on regular home visits) and were born at term (37 to 42 weeks gestation), in addition they were of known birth weight determined within 24 hours of birth. Details of the one-third of births not satisfying these criteria are not given, but they are rigorous and highly selective. Among the 288 births included in the analysis, the mothers were categorized according to their total supplementary caloric intake throughout pregnancy. There was a clear gradient in birth weight rising regularly from low users to moderate users to high users of supplement.

This analysis departs from the initial experimental design and depends instead on differences in birth weight among women self-selected for different levels of caloric intake. No important confounding factors that could have been introduced by self-selection, however, were discovered by the analytic control for a number of variables including maternal height, weight early in pregnancy, attendance at the centre, parity, interval since last birth, maternal illness, incidence of intra-uterine infection (as judged from neonatal cord blood IgM levels) maternal age and length of gestation. The claim of the investigators that total amount of supplementation irrespective of the trimester of its ingestion affected birth weight outcome does not seem to be substantiated by the data published so far. In addition, the claim that the effect of increased calories occurred irrespective of its source in either carbohydrate or protein is also not made entirely clear by the data published.

Despite the limitations of the data published to date, these results are persuasive of a causal connection between dietary intake and birth weight among women drawn from a chronically malnourished population who can carry their pregnancies to term. Even though the women are self-selected for dietary intake, the most obvious confounding factors have been ruled out. Judgement must be reserved, however, until full analysis of the whole and not a selected sample can be studied.

A seventh experimental study was recently completed among a poor black population in New York City[63]. The Harlem Prenatal Project aimed to test whether food supplements, begun no later than the 30th week of pregnancy, might raise birth weight, and other indices of fetal and infant growth and development. Participants were selected to be at high risk of bearing growth-retarded infants (but free of known medical causes of low birth weight), and were randomly allocated in partial double blind fashion to three groups. Two nutritional supplements differed in protein and caloric content, but were packaged in identical cans and bore identical labels, and to which supplement a woman was assigned was unknown to her or the staff. The third group, assigned to regular clinic treatment without beverage supplements, were of course not blind to their treatment assignment.

Analyses are as yet preliminary for the approximately 750 women who successfully completed the treatment regimen, but some conclusions seem justified:

(1) There was no significant increase in birth weight in the treated populations taken as a whole.

(2) Some sub-groups benefited, others did worse.

(a) Those at highest risk of having low birth weight infants (smokers, and women of lowest pre-pregnant weight) had higher birth weight than controls, especially among those carrying to term.

(b) The most striking treatment effect was a reversal of the depressed weight gain and birth weight associated with heavy smoking. Among controls, smoking during pregnancy was associated with lower maternal weight gain and infant birth weight, with a steep gradient with increased smoking[64].

The early stage of analysis of these complex outcomes does not permit a firm conclusion, and makes impossible as yet any generalization for clinical and public health practice.

PRENATAL NUTRITION AND MENTAL COMPETENCE

PHASE OF DEVELOPMENT AND MENTAL COMPETENCE: ANIMAL STUDIES

The animal and human evidence discussed above related only to the first two sequences of the following postulated causal chain: Critical period nutritional deficiency → retarded brain growth → permanent organic impairment of brain → persisting mental effects. The assumption that impaired brain growth caused by nutritional deficiency is expressed in functional deficits in mental performance is not secure. In animals, some relevant studies discussed above have demonstrated organic impairment, and others have demonstrated learning deficits or behaviour change. The crucial experiments will need to demonstrate that all these effects occur together and in sequence under the same experimental conditions. In humans, some autopsy studies suggest, as indicated above, that prenatal malnutrition retards the growth of the brain and other organs. Other studies suggest that early childhood malnutrition also retards brain growth. In addition, some studies suggest also that early childhood malnutrition retards later mental performance, but some do not. So far no study provides the knowledge that brain impairment is an intervening factor in the causal chain leading from nutrition to mental competence. Autopsy at death cannot prove the irreversibility of the brain cell depletion reported in fatal cases of early malnutrition, nor indeed can we know from such studies whether the depletion is compatible with life and ever to be found in survivors; nor, if the depletion is compatible with life, what effect on the mental competence of survivors would be.

We must therefore turn to evidence that indirectly supports the postulated causal sequence. The additional evidence bears on the effects of nutritional deprivation on mental competence and behaviour. We shall first review relevant animal experiments and then, in succeeding chapters, the relevant human observational studies.

Animal nutritional deprivation experiment is a rapidly growing field. The use of a variety of animals, a variety of methods of depriving them of nutrients, and a variety of outcome measures leads one to anticipate a variety of results. Most of the experiments have been on rats. Since the main part of the rat brain growth spurt occurs during suckling, postnatal deprivation provides a reasonable test of critical period hypotheses. The nutritional deprivation is achieved either through the mothers' diet or through the milk supplied to the young in lactation. According to design, mothers are fed scanty balanced diets or diets unbalanced in some constituents (usually protein) before, during or after pregnancy. Milk supply may also be reduced by curtailing suckling time, or by manipulating litter size through random allocation of varying numbers of offspring to lactating mothers.

All these manipulations are likely to alter the environment of the suckling test animals as well as their nutrient supply. Undernourished mothers do not treat their offspring in the same manner as wellnourished mothers, and their nurturing seems to be less effective. In addition, the social milieu of large and small litters is not the same; for instance, competition for the dam's nipples or for her attention is bound to be more intense in large than in small litters. Hence observed maternal nutrition in animals can be the result of mother–child interaction or social milieu rather than of the deficient nutrition of the offspring.

The effects studied in nutritional experiments have been grouped under the five headings of (1) developmental delays, (2) activity level, (3) response to food, (4) response to stressors, and (5) learning ability[65]. Recent studies have paid special attention to the modification of such effects by the social situation[66, 67].

Nutritional experiments with rats have induced delay in the development of reflexes and of simple behaviour patterns including exploratory behaviour and motor ability[68–73]. Such effects may be transient, and the consequences in adulthood of lags in early development cannot be predicted.

In adult rats poorly nourished in early life, exploratory activity in novel surroundings seems to be reduced on initial exposure, but it increases on continued exposure over long periods[65]. This increased exploratory activity is found with food incentives[74], but other forms of activity sustained over long periods, like that on 'running wheels', are also increased[75]. Exaggerated responses made by hungry rats to stimuli and situations involving food[71, 72, 74], however, suggest that they have an altered level of motivation about food, which may flow from either psychological or metabolic changes. Exaggerated responses to food are also found in rhesus monkeys. When spurred by rewards of food, starved monkeys learn more quickly than controls[67]. These changes in 'hunger drive' complicate the interpretation of learning experiments.

Overreaction to stressors other than food also occurs in animals exposed to early malnutrition. In undernourished rats, loud bangs reduced movement in an 'open field' as compared with controls; electric shocks inhibited behaviour or induced avoidance more than they did in controls[66, 71, 72]. Malnourished nesting mothers emit a higher rate of ultrasonic sounds when her offspring are interfered with[76]. The behaviour of pigs and rhesus monkeys can be similarly interpreted as overreactive[77, 67]. In rats, such exaggerated responses are coherent with the finding of raised corticosterone levels in the blood[78].

Studies of the effects of nutrition on learning ability must clearly be approached with caution because of possible confounding by nutritional effects on other behaviour. Strength of hunger drive and level of initial deprivation might confound experiments where the stimulus is aversive. Moreover, the measures of learning themselves are problematic as valid indicators of general mental competence. In addition to the difficulties of analogy with human tests, correlations between separate tests are likely to be poor[79].

On the whole, the balance among the inconsistent results is in favour of an adverse effect of early malnutrition on learning. Many tests of associative learning, including reversals, reveal no disadvantage for the malnourished. More complex tests, however, are more suggestive of the adverse effects of early malnutrition. Thus Turkewitz, working with Stewart's strain of rats malnourished over several generations, found increasing disparities between experimental and control rats as the complexity of the learning task increased[80]. Zimmerman, Strobel, Steere and Geist, who worked with rhesus monkeys, could detect no disparity in a wide range of learning tasks, but did detect a disparity in 'discrimination reversal learning', in which they suggested a deficit in attention might be involved[67]. Disparities in learning ability related to early nutrition, however, have proved sensitive to social situation. Thus among rats, nutritional effects found in small litters have not emerged in larger litters, and in rhesus monkeys effects found in those reared in isolation have not emerged among those reared in groups[67, 81].

To summarize the results of animal studies, it is probable that nutritional deficiency of sufficient duration during critical growth periods

retards brain growth, and that such growth retardation may be irre-
coverable. It is less certain that this organic impairment is expressed
in functional deficits, either in learning ability or in other behaviour.
Behaviour other than learning has more often been influenced by nutritional deprivation than has learning itself; rhesus monkeys with induced
kwashiorkor-like syndromes show striking changes in response to food,
and unadaptive reactions to unpleasant and to novel stimuli. In experiments that expose pregnant or suckling mothers of other species to
undernutrition, some of the changed behaviour in the offspring could
arise from changed behaviour in the mothers induced by the conditions
of the experiment, rather than from a direct effect of nutrition on the
developing organism. In addition, learning and behavioural manifestations following early nutritional deprivation have proved sensitive to
social milieu. These results could point to interaction between the
effects of nutritional deprivation and social situation, or to interaction
between the socialization process of the young and social situation.
They are not conclusive.

FETAL GROWTH, AND MENTAL DEVELOPMENT: HUMAN STUDIES

The human brain develops considerably during gestation. We have
noted the marked growth in brain mass in the late fetal period, and
the inference from autopsy studies that this growth can be retarded
by prenatal nutritional deficiency. Evidence that poor nutrition during
pregnancy has a sequel in depressed mental performance in the offspring,
however, has been confusing. In human beings it is rarely possible to
separate entirely experiences of malnutrition in the prenatal period
from those of the postnatal period. One reason is that children of
mothers malnourished while pregnant seldom have optimum diets in
postnatal life. They cannot be fostered at random, in favourable and
unfavourable nutritional conditions, as experimental animals have been.

The view that prenatal nutrition affects development of the central
nervous system is consistent with some studies of congenital anomalies.
In West Germany, the frequency of malformations of the central
nervous system rose during the food shortages after World War II and
fell when conditions improved[82]. In the United States, too, a rise and
fall in the incidence of anencephaly has run parallel to the level of living
conditions and among salient changes in living conditions, prenatal

nutrition is one that must be considered[83]. But it is one among many factors that changed concomitantly with the incidence of anomaly.

Studies of twins point indirectly to effects of intrauterine nutrition on intelligence. On average, the heavier twin has most often, if not always, been found superior on intelligence test scores[84, 85]. Since duration of gestation (as well as genetic predisposition, in the case of uniovular twins) is held constant in twin comparisons, the differences in birth weight between pairs have been attributed to differences in intrauterine nutrition mediated by the arrangement of the blood supply to the twin fetuses. Other types of studies also suggest that the internal disposition of nutrients by the vascular supply through the placenta is a cause of retarded fetal growth[86-91]. Low birth weight in twins may thus be part of a sequence in which deficiency in nutrients reaching the fetus leads to depressed intelligence in childhood.

Many studies suggest that low birth weight is an antecedent of reduced mental competence[92, 93], the lower the birth weight, the greater mental handicap tends to be[94]. All these observations taken together show that poor nutrition, low birth weight and mental retardation are associated under certain conditions. The simplest assumption is that poor maternal nutrition causes low birth weight, and that low birth weight leads to brain impairment and mental retardation. But the nature of the links are far from clear. Figures 3.6 and 3.7 illustrate some of the possible connections[4].

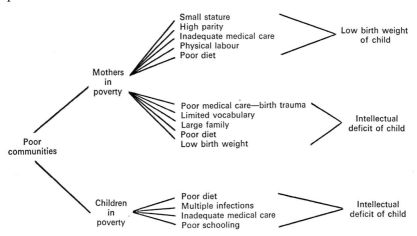

Figure 3.6 Some confounding variables that may affect birthweight and intellect. (Taken from Stein, Z., Susser, M., Saenger, G. and Marolla, F. (1975) [40])

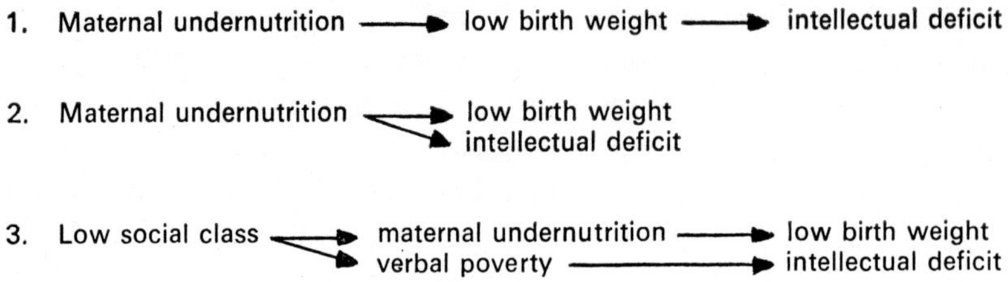

1. Maternal undernutrition ———▶ low birth weight ———▶ intellectual deficit

2. Maternal undernutrition ⟨ low birth weight
                              intellectual deficit

3. Low social class ⟨ maternal undernutrition ———▶ low birth weight
                       verbal poverty ———————————▶ intellectual deficit

Figure 3.7 Diagram of three among many possible causal paths between maternal undernutrition, low birth weight, and intellectual deficit. (Taken from Stein, Z., Susser, M., Saenger, G. and Marolla, F. (1975) [40])

In Figure 3.7 are listed some common attributes of mothers and children living in poverty that might contribute to low birth weight or to mental retardation. A 'case' either of low birth weight or of mental retardation is more likely to have the listed attributes than a 'control'. A case of low birth weight is therefore also more likely than a control to be of low birth weight. Thus an association of low birth weight with mental retardation may be found in the presence of any of their shared attributes and could have a common cause in that attribute. For the present, low birth weight cannot unequivocally be assigned a causal or even a mediating role in mental retardation.

Low birth weight itself has heterogeneous causes, known and unknown. Its association with mental retardation is reduced when those cases are excluded in which the causes of mental retardation are known to antedate birth weight and retard development, as with Down's anomaly. When very low birth weight (under 1500 g) is the precursor of mental retardation, pre-existing congenital defects seem largely to account for both the low birth weight and the mental retardation.[93] Where congenital defect does not accompany very low birth weight, one study suggests that brain damage may be a necessary intervening factor between small size and mental retardation, at least where the small size reflects a short period of gestation. The frequency of cerebral palsy was high among those with short gestation periods, and the frequency of mental retardation was raised only among those with cerebral palsy[95]. One presumed causal sequence (among many) is thus premature birth→very low birth weight→cerebral damage→mental retardation.

With moderately low birth weight, the nature of the association with mental competence is even less clear. The way in which the postulated causal factors of low birth weight and retarded mental development are interconnected obfuscates the causal sequence among them. The consistent social class gradients of birth weight and intelligence quotient are sharp and parallel, to the disadvantage of the lower classes. Yet when the closest possible control of social class has been applied, by making sib comparisons within families, only a small difference in intelligence quotient has been found between sibs of different birth weight (excepting the few sibships with gross weight differences between members)[96].

This finding suggests that among the complex of variables associated with social class, differences between families and not birth weight differences between individuals are the likely intervening link between social environment and measured intelligence. Similarly, it has been shown that within families with a mildly retarded child, the affected child is no more likely than his sibs to have been of moderately low birth weight or small for the period of gestation[96-98]. These studies are in accord with the conclusion that cultural–familial retardation depends on membership in families of distinctive character and milieu.

The distinction between organic impairment and dysfunction may be at the root of the apparent incoherence of the relationship of mental performance with low birth weight. Many factors that limit or enhance function and influence levels of disability act postnatally.

Prenatal factors which cause mild impairment might be overshadowed or compensated for by acquired functional abilities. Compensation may occur only in favourable circumstances—in other words, there would then be interaction between the prenatal factors and postnatal learning. Some studies, but not all, point to interaction between the effects of low birth weight and social class to produce mental retardation[93, 95, 99-101]. In these, moderately low birth weight was associated with mild mental retardation or lowered intelligence quotient only among the lower classes and not among the higher. In short, moderately low birth weight seems to be neither a sufficient nor a necessary cause of mild mental retardation, but it may well be a contributory cause in unfavourable circumstances.

MENTAL COMPETENCE AFTER PRENATAL EXPOSURE TO FAMINE

Our own studies of the Dutch famine of 1944/45 provide the only available data with which to test the hypothesis that prenatal nutrition in humans affects subsequent mental performance. The main data source is the record of medical and psychological examinations made at the military induction of all males in the Netherlands at 19 years of age[40, 102, 103]. The population under study at induction comprised over 100000 males born in the selected famine and control cities in the 3-year period January 1, 1944 to December 31, 1946. Some severely handicapped men (0.6%) were excused from attending the induction examination in person, but they were entered on the induction records. In such cases, an assessment of their condition was made from the clinical record forwarded to the induction centre by a medical practitioner.

In this study, we placed reliance on psychometric indices as the dependent variables most likely to detect a famine effect. The psychometric index of greatest sensitivity and most importance is the Raven Progressive Matrices.

Clinical assessments were also studied. The clinical levels of severe and mild retardation in the data of the military induction examination are consistent with usual standards—that is, a division around IQ 50 separates the two levels of severity. The two conditions were defined in terms of the clinical diagnosis assigned at the induction examination. Diagnoses used were coded for the record according to the International Classification of Diseases (ICD) of the World Health Organization (1948). Severe mental retardation includes the codes for idiocy (3250), imbecility (3251), mongolism (3254), and all others (3255); mild mental retardation covers the codes moron (3252) and borderline intelligence (3253). All those allocated these codes were included in the analysis, whether the diagnoses were given as a primary or as a secondary cause of rejection for military service.

RAVEN PROGRESSIVE MATRICES

No variation in Raven scores in association with prenatal exposure to famine, either early or late in gestation, is detectable. A numerically higher Raven score signifies a poorer performance. The D2 cohort, conceived at the height of the famine, actually bettered the performance of other cohorts on the Raven test (that is, the D2 numerical score was lower). This was a consequence of the effect of famine, not on mental performance, but on fertility.

By far the most striking variation is between the mean scores of the non-manual and manual classes (Figure 3.8). The influence of the social class variable is underlined by the sensitivity of Raven scores to differential fertility among the social classes. The D2 cohort owed its improved mean score to the altered proportions of the social classes in that cohort; we were able to show that in this cohort the fertility of the manual classes had fallen more than that of the non-manual social classes. The slight advantage maintained by the D2 cohort in each of the two classes analysed in Figure 3.8 disappeared in an analysis of nine occupational classes.

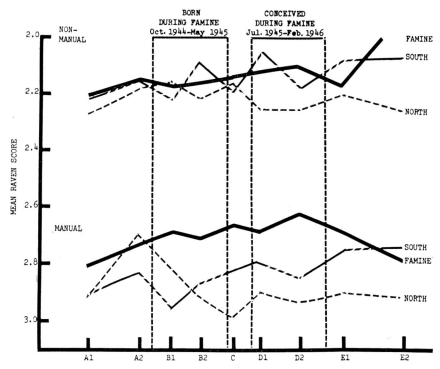

Figure 3.8 Raven scores by area and class (mean Raven scores by cohort in famine, Northern control, and Southern control areas, comparing manual and non-manual occupational classes). (Taken from Stein, Z., Susser, M., Saenger, G. and Marolla, F. (1975) [40])

MILD MENTAL RETARDATION

There is a huge disparity among social classes in the frequency of mild mental retardation. In Figure 3.9, therefore, we show prevalence among classes divided from the outset by manual and non-manual occupations. As expected, sons of fathers in manual work had far higher rates of mild mental retardation than sons of fathers in non-manual work. The overall rates among social classes were much more dissimilar than those among areas.

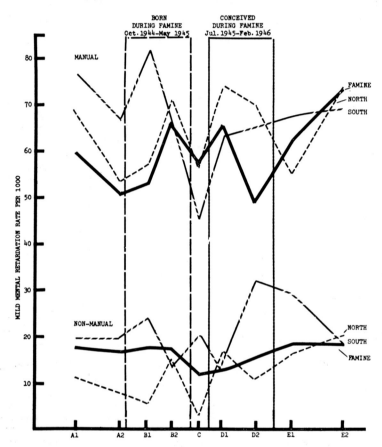

Figure 3.9 Mild mental retardation by area and social class (rates of mild mental retardation, per 1000 total births by cohort in famine, Northern control, and Southern control areas, comparing manual and non-manual occupational classes). (Taken from Stein, Z., Susser, M., Saenger, G. and Marolla, F. (1975) [40])

Variation in the prevalence of mild mental retardation was related neither to conception nor to birth during the famine. In comparisons by place, prevalence in famine and control cities was similar among both social classes. In comparisons by time also, there is no consistent relation of prevalence of mild mental retardation with prenatal exposure to famine. Among the manual working class in the famine area, the rise in prevalence in the B2 cohort, born at the height of the famine, is matched in the North and exceeded by the rise in the E2 cohort conceived and born after the famine. The decline in the D2 cohort, conceived at the height of the famine, is analogous with that of the Raven Progressive Matrices in the same cohort and can be accounted for by the pattern of differential fertility among the social classes during the famine.

SEVERE MENTAL RETARDATION

The frequency of severe mental retardation among survivors of the birth cohorts is related neither to conception nor to birth during the famine (Figure 3.10).

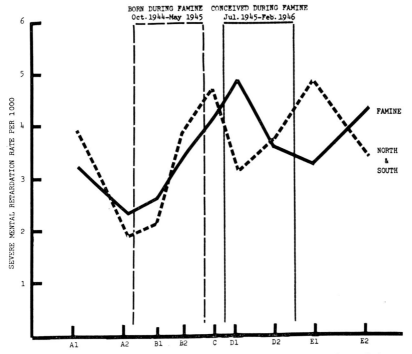

Figure 3.10 Severe mental retardation by area (rates of severe mental retardation per 1000 total births by cohort: famine area and combined Northern and Southern control areas). Taken from Stein, Z., Susser, M., Saenger, G. and Marolla, F. (1975) [40])

Thus several measures of mental performance in a national population of young men at military induction show no effect of prenatal exposure to famine. The measures of mental performance analysed include 5 tests (Raven Progressive Matrices; Language Comprehension; Arithmetic; Clerical Aptitude; Bennett Test of Mechanical Comprehension) and a score combining the results of all tests. Only one test, the Raven Progressive Matrices, is presented and discussed in detail, but all tests are in agreement with regard to the absence of a famine effect. In addition, the prevalence of mild and of severe mental retardation was analysed and similarly showed no famine effect. We also sought evidence of interaction of prenatal famine exposure with indices of social environment that might have influenced compensatory learning opportunities and subsequent mental performance. No such evidence was found in analyses of social class, religious affiliation, family size, and birth order. We explored the relation of measures of mental performance to famine-induced mortality in order to test the explanation that selective survival might have masked or distorted an association of prenatal famine exposure with mental competence. No distortion was apparent, and this alternative hypothesis can be dismissed.

A precise test of the hypothesis that birth weight is a contributory factor in mental performance should discriminate between prenatal phases in order to define critical periods. In the study of the Dutch famine, it was possible to search for consequences of nutritional deprivation at postulated critical periods with some precision of timing. Both the phase of development at which successive birth cohorts were exposed to famine, and the duration of their exposure, could be derived from the data.

The results of the study of the Dutch famine can be summarized as follows:

1. Above a threshold value of food intake a mother probably affords the fetus protection from nutritional deprivation. Thus, when everyday diets are reasonably adequate extra nutritional intake may not affect the fetus.
2. Below a nutritional threshold the fetus is vulnerable to some extent in the third trimester of gestation in terms of intrauterine growth and early posnatal mortality. Of the fetal dimensions reported weight has seemed most sensitive to nutritional effects and length

and head size less sensitive. Slowed fetal growth was a mediating factor between prenatal nutritional deprivation and raised death rate in the first three months of life.

3. Prenatal brain cell depletion in fetuses exposed during the third trimester to maternal starvation probably occurs. If it occurs this outcome points to great resilience on the part of surviving fetuses, for organic impairment did not become manifest in this function.
4. Among adult survivors we have found no evidence that prenatal nutrition affects mental competence.

Finally, we believe we must accept that poor prenatal nutrition cannot be considered a factor in the social distribution of mental competence among surviving adults in industrial societies. This is not to exclude a possible effect of prenatal nutritional deprivation in combination with poor postnatal nutrition, especially in pre-industrial societies, but the information to confirm that is not yet in. This last possibility is given greater salience by the apparent effect of nutritional supplements on fetal growth observed in the Guatemala studies, as well as by two observations not discussed in the main body of this paper. We have mentioned the recent studies of Dobbing which indicate a continued rapid growth of the brain through the second year of life. This continuing postnatal growth comprises some 80–90% of the total period of the brain growth spurt. Hence one must look to the effects of postnatal nutritional deprivation in severely malnourished populations to seek out the possible effects of nutrition on mental competence. The two best studies so far carried out show that this too is a difficult endeavour, since their results conflict. One of these at least points to effects on mental competence, up to pubescence, of postnatal malnutrition in interaction with adverse social environment.

REFERENCES

1. Knobloch, H. and Pasamanick, B. (1962). Mental subnormality: Medical progress. *N. Engl. J. Med.*, **266**, 1045–1051, 1092–1096, 1155–1161
2. Cravioto, J., De Licardie M. S. and Birch, H. G. (1966). Nutrition, growth and neurointegrative development: An experimental and ecological study. *Pediatrics*, **38** (Suppl.): 319
3. Winick, M. (1969). Malnutrition and brain development. *J. Pediatr.*, **74**, 667

4. Stein, Z. A. and Kassab, H. (1970). Nutrition. In *Mental Retardation*, II. (J. Wortis, editor) p. 92 (New York: Grune and Stratton)

5. Lewis, E. O. (1933). Types of mental deficiency and their social significance. *Ment. Sci.*, **79**, 298

6. Roberts, J. A. F. (1952) The genetics of mental deficiency. *Eugen. Rev.*, **44**, 71

7. Stein, Z. A., and Susser, M. W. (1963). The social distribution of mental retardation. *Amer. J. Ment. Def.*, **67**, 811

8. Birch, H. G. and Gussow, J. D. (1970) *Disadvantaged Children: Health, Nutrition and School Failure.* (New York: Harcourt, Brace and World)

9. Rutter, M., Graham, P. and Yule, W. (1970). *A Neuro-psychiatric Study in Childhood* (Clinics in Developmental Medicine Nos. 35/36). (London: William Heinemann Medical Books)

10. Winick, M. and Noble, A. (1966). Cellular response in rats during malnutrition at various ages. *J. Nutr.*, **89**, 300

11. Zamenhof, S., van Marthens, E. and Margolis, F. L. (1968). DNA (cell number) and protein in neonatal brain: Alteration by maternal dietary protein restriction. *Science (N.Y.)*, **160**, 322

12. Dobbing, J. (1964). The influence of early nutrition on the development of the brain. *Proc. R. Soc. (Biol.)*, **159**, 503

13. Platt, B. S. and Stewart, R. J. C. (1969). Effect of protein-calorie deficiency on dogs. II. Morphological changes in the nervous system. *Develop. Med. Child. Neurol.*, **11**, 174

14. Dobbing, J. (1968). Vulnerable Periods in Developing Brain. In *Applied Neurochemistry*. (A. N. Davison and J. Dobbing editors). (London and Oxford: Blackwell Scientific Publishers)

15. McCance, R. A. and Widdowson, E. M. (1974). Review lecture: The determinants of growth and form. *Proc. R. Soc. Lond. (Biol.)*, **185**, 1

16. Platt, B. S. and Stewart, R. J. C. (1971). Reversible and irreversible effects of protein-calorie deficiency on the central nervous system of animals and man. *Wld Rev. Nutr. Diet*, **13**, 43

17. Fish, I. and Winick, M. (1969). Effect of malnutrition on regional growth of the developing rat brain. *Exp. Neurol.*, **25**, 534

18. Dobbing, J. (1974). The later growth of the brain and its vulnerability. *Pediatrics*, **53**, 2

19. Dobbing, J. and Sands, J. (1973). Quantitative growth and development of human brain. *Arch. Dis. Childh.*, **48**, 757

20. Winick, M., Brasel, J. A. and Rosso, P. (1972). Nutrition and cell growth. In *Nutrition and Development*, p. 49 (M. Winick, editor) (New York: John Wiley and Sons)

21. Bergner, L. and Susser, M. W. (1970). Low birthweight and prenatal nutrition: An interpretative review. *Pediatrics*, **46**, 946

22. Winick, M. and Rosso, P. (1969). Head circumference and cell growth of the brain in normal and marasmic children. *J. Pediatr.*, **74**, 774

23. Brasel, J. (1974). Prenatal malnutrition in humans. In *Nutrition and*

Fetal Development, Vol. 2, Current Concepts in Nutrition, (M. Winick, editor) p. 21. (New York: John Wiley and Sons)

24. Winick, M. (1970). Nutrition and nerve cell growth. *Fed. Proc.*, **29**, 1510
25. Butler, N. R. and Bonham, D. G. (1963). *Perinatal Mortality: The First Report of the 1958 British Perinatal Mortality Survey Under the Auspices of the National Birthday Trust Fund*. (Edinburgh: Livingstone)
26. Brimblecombe, F. S. and Ashford, J. R. (1968). Significance of low birth weight in perinatal mortality: A study of variations within England and Wales. *Br. J. Prev. Soc. Med.*, **22**, 27
27. Susser, M. W., Marolla, F. A., and Fleiss, J. (1972). Birthweight, fetal age and perinatal mortality. *Am. J. Epidem.*, **96**, 197
28. McGanity, W. J., Cannon, R. O., Bridgforth, E. B., Martin, M. P., Densen, P. M., Newbill, J. A., McClellan, G. S., Christie, A., Peterson, J. C. and Darby, W. J. (1954). The Vanderbilt cooperative study of maternal and infant nutrition. VI. Relationship of obstetric performance to nutrition. *Am. J. Obstet. Gynecol.*, **67**, 501
29. McGanity, W. J., Cannon, R. O., Bridgforth, E. B., Martin, M. P., Densen, P. M., Newbill, J. A., McClellan, G. S., Christie, A., Peterson, J. C., and Darby, W. J. (1954). The Vanderbilt cooperative study of maternal and infant nutrition. V. Description and outcome of obstetrics sample. *Am. J. Obstet. Gynecol.*, **67**, 491
30. Thomson, A. M. (1958). Diet in pregnancy. 1. Dietary survey technique and the nutritive value of diets taken by primigravidae. *Br. J. Nutr.*, **12**, 446
31. Thomson, A. M. (1959). Diet in pregnancy. 2. Assessment of the nutritive value of diets, especially in relation to differences between social classes. *Br. J. Nutr.*, **13**, 190
32. Thomson, A. M. (1963). Prematurity: Socio-economic and nutritional factors. *Mod. Prob. Pediatr.*, **8**, 197
33. Thomson, A. M. and Hytten, F. E. (1961). Caloric requirements in human pregnancy. *Proc. Nutr. Soc.*, **20**, 76
34. Thomson, A. M. and I. Leitch. (1971). *The Physiology of Human Pregnancy*. (Oxford: Blackwell Scientific Publications)
35. Rush, D., Stein, Z., and Susser, M. (unpublished).
36. Salisbury, H. (1970). *The 900 Days*. (New York: Aron Books)
37. Antonov, A. N. (1947). Children born during siege of Leningrad in 1942. *J. Pediatr.*, **30**, 250
38. McCance, R. A., Widdowson, E. M., Dean, R. F. A. and Thrussell, L. A. (1951). *Studies of Undernutrition, Wuppertal 1946–9*. Medical Research Council Special Series No. 275. (London: His Majesty's Stationery Office)
39. Smith, C. A. (1947). Effects of wartime starvation in Holland on pregnancy and its products. *Amer. J. Obstet. Gynecol.*, **53**, 599–608
40. Stein, Z., Susser, M., Saenger, G. and Marolla, F. (1975). *Famine and Human Development: The Dutch Hunger Winter of 1944–45*. (New York: Oxford University Press)

41. Stein, Z. and Susser, M. (1975). The Dutch famine, 1944–1945, and the reproductive process. I. Effects on six indices at birth, *Pediatr. Res.*, **9**, 70

42. Stein, Z. and Susser, M. (1975). The Dutch famine, 1944–1945, and the reproductive process. II. Interrelations of caloric rations and six indices at birth. *Pediatr. Res.*, **9**, 76

43. Ryan, C. (1974). *A Bridge Too far.* (New York: Simon and Schuster)

44. Stoch, M. B. and Smythe, P. M. (1963). Does undernutrition during infancy inhibit growth and subsequent intellectual development? *Arch. Dis. Childh.*, **38**, 546

45. Monckeberg, F. (1968). Effect of early marasmic malnutrition on subsequent physical and psychological development. In *Malnutrition, Learning, and Behavior*, (N. S. Scrimshaw and J. E. Gordon, editors) p. 269 (Cambridge, Massachusetts: M.I.T. Press)

46. Chase, H. P. and Martin, H. P. (1970). Undernutrition and child development. *N. Engl. J. Med.*, **282**, 933

47. Gruenwald, P. and Minh, H. N. (1961). Evaluation of body and organ weights in perinatal pathology. II. Weight of body and placenta of surviving and autopsied infants. *Am. J. Obstet. Gynecol.*, **82**, 312

48. Gruenwald, P. (1966). Growth of the human fetus. I. Normal growth and its variation. *Am. J. Obstet. Gynecol.*, **94**, 1112

49. Naeye, R. L. (1970). Structural correlates of fetal undernutrition. In *Fetal Growth and Development* (H. W. Waisman and G. R. Kerr, editors) p. 241 (New York: McGraw-Hill)

50. Nelson, K. B. and J. Deutschberger. (1970). Head size at one year as a predictor of four-year I.Q. *Develop. Med. Child. Neurol.*, **12**, 487

51. Baum, J. D. and Searls, D. (1971). Head shape and size of pre-term low-birthweight infants. *Develop. Med. Child. Neurol.*, **13**, 576

52. Davies, P. A. and Davies, J. P. (1970). Very low birthweight and subsequent head growth. *Lancet*, **ii**, 1216

53. Brown, R. E. (1965). Decreased brain weight in malnutrition and its implications. *E. Afr., Med. J.*, **42**, 584

54. Penrose, L. S. (1962). *Biology of Mental Defect.* 2nd Ed. (New York: Grune and Stratton)

55. Martin, H. P. (1970). Microcephaly and mental retardation. *Am. J. Dis. Childh.*, **119**, 128

56. Stein, Z., Susser, M. and Sturmans, F. (1975). Famine and mortality. *T. Soc. Geneesk.*, **53**, 134, 159

57. Interim report of People's League of Health. (1942). Nutrition of expectant and nursing mothers. *Lancet*, **ii**, 10

58. Ebbs, J. H., Tisdall, F. F. and Scott, W. A. (1941). The Influence of prenatal diet on the mother and child. *J. Nutr.*, **22**, 515

59. Cameron, C. S. and Graham, S. (1944). Antenatal diet and its influence on stillbirths and prematurity. *Glasgow Med. J.*, **142**, 1

60. Dieckman, W. J., Adain, F. L., Michel, H., Kiamen, S., Dunkle, F., Arthur, B., Costin, M., Campbell, A., Wensley, A. C. and Lorang, E.

(1944). Calcium, phosphorus, iron and nitrogen balance in pregnant women. *Amer. J. Obstet. Gynecol.*, **47**, 357

61. Tompkins, W. T., Mitchell, R. McN. and Wiehl, D. G. (1955). *Maternal and Newborn Nutrition Studies at Philadelphia Lying-in Hospital. Maternal Studies.* II. *Prematurity and Maternal Nutrition.* The Promotion of Maternal and Newborn Health. Milbank Memorial Fund, New York, p. 230

62. Habicht, J.-P., Yarbrough, C., Lechtig, A. and Klein, R. E. (1974). Relation of maternal supplementary feeding during pregnancy to birth weight and other sociobiological factors. In *Nutrition and Fetal Development*, Vol. 2, Current Concepts in Nutrition, (M. Winick, editor) p. 147 (New York: Wiley)

63. Rush, D., Stein, Z., Christakis, G., and Susser, M. (1974). The Prenatal Project: The first 20 months of operation. In *Nutrition and Fetal Development*, Vol. 2, Current Concepts in Nutrition (M. Winick, editor), p. 95 (New York: Wiley)

64. Rush, D. (1974). Examination of the relationship between birthweight, cigarette smoking during pregnancy and maternal weight gain. *Br. J. Obstet. Gynaecol.*, **81**, 746

65. Dobbing, J. and Smart, J. L. (1973). Early undernutrition, brain development and behaviour. In *Clinics in Developmental Medicine*, No. 47, Ethology and Development. (S. A. Barnett, editor) (London: Heinemann)

66. Levitsky, D. A. and Barnes, R. H. (1970). Effects of early malnutrition on reaction of adult rats to aversive stimuli. *Nature (London)*, **225**, 468

67. Zimmermann, R. R., Strobel, D. A., Steere, P. and Geist, C. R. (1973). Behaviour and malnutrition in the Rhesus monkey. In *Primate Behavior*. (L. Rosenblum, editor) (New York: Academic Press)

68. Cowley, J. J. and Griesel, R. D. (1959). Some effects of a low protein diet on a first filial generation of white rats. *J. Genet. Psychol.*, **95**, 187

69. Frankova, S. and Barnes, R. H. (1968). Influence of malnutrition in early life on exploratory behaviour of rats .*J. Nutr.*, **96**, 477

70. Simonson, M., Sherwin, R. W., Anilane, J. K., Yu, W. Y. and Chow, B. F. (1969). Neuromotor development in progeny of underfed mother rats. *J. Nutr.*, **98**, 18

71. Smart, J. L. and Dobbing, J. (1971). Vulnerability of developing brain. II. Effects of early nutritional deprivation on reflex ontogeny and development of behavior in the rat. *Brain Res.*, **28**, 85

72. Smart, J. L. and Dobbing, J. (1971). Vulnerability of developing brain. VI. Relative effects of fetal and early postnatal undernutrition on reflex ontogeny and development of behavior in the rat. *Brain Res.*, **33**, 303

73. Altman, J., Sudarshan, K., Das, G. D., McCormick, N. and Barnes, D. (1971). The influence of nutrition on neural and behavioral development. III. Development of some motor, particularly locomotor patterns during infancy. *Dev. Psychobiol.*, **4**, 97

74. Barnes, R. H., Moore, A. U., Reid, I. M. and Pond, W. G. (1968). Effect

of food deprivation on behavioral patterns. In *Malnutrition, Learning, and Behavior*, (N. S. Scrimshaw, editor) p. 203 (Cambridge, Massachusetts: M.I.T. Press)

75. Guthrie, H. A. and Brown, M. L. (1968). Effect of severe undernutrition in early life on growth, brain size and composition in adult rats. *J. Nutr.*, **94**, 419

76. Bell, R. W. (1973). Interactive effects of variable population density and dietary protein sufficiency upon selected morphological, neurochemical, and behavioral attributes in the rat. In *Nutrition and Mental Functions*, (G. Serban, editor) p. 91 (New York: Plenum Press)

77. Barnes, R. H., Moore, A. U. and Pond, W. G. (1970). Behavioral abnormalities in young adult pigs caused by malnutrition in early life. *J. Nutr.*, **100**, 149

78. Adlard, B. P. and Smart, J. L. (1971). Plasma 11-hydroxy corticosteroid concentrations in stressed adult rats after undernutrition in early life. *Biochem. J.*, **125**, 12P-13P

79. Searle, L. V. (1949). The organization of hereditary maze-brightness and maze-dullness. *Genet. Psychol. Mon.*, **39**, 279

80. Turkewitz, G. (1973). Learning in chronically protein-deprived rats. In *Nutrition and Mental Functions*, p. 113 (New York: Plenum Press)

81. Levitsky, D. (1973). Malnutrition and animal models of cognitive development. In *Nutrition and Mental Functions* (G. Serban, editor) p. 75 (New York: Plenum Press)

82. Eichmann, E. and Gesenius, H. (1952). Die Missgeburtenzunahme in Berlin and Umgebung in den Nachkriegsjahren. *Arch. Gynak.*, **181**, 168

83. Naggan, L. (1969). The recent decline in the prevalence of anencephaly and spina bifida. *Am. J. Epidem.*, **89**, 154

84. Churchill, J. A. (1965). The relationship between intelligence and birthweight in twins. *Neurology*, **15**, 341

85. Kaelber, C. T. and Pugh, T. F. (1969). Influence of intrauterine relations on the intelligence of twins. *N. Engl. J. Med.*, **280**, 1030

86. Gibson, J. R. and McKeown, T. (1950). Observations on all births (23,970), in Birmingham, 1947. I. Duration of gestation. *Br. J. Social Med.*, **4**, 221

87. Gibson, J. R. and McKeown, T. (1951). Observations on all births (23,970), in Birmingham, 1947. III. Survival. *Br. J. Social Med.*, **5**, 177

88. McKeown, T. and Gibson, J. R. (1951). Observations on all births (23,970), in Birmingham, 1947. II. Birth weight. *Br. J. Social Med.*, **5**, 98

89. McLaren, A. and Michie, D. (1963). Nature of the systemic effect of litter size on gestation period in mice. *J. Reprod. Fertil.*, **6**, 139

90. Payne, P. R. and Wheeler, E. F. (1967). Growth of the foetus. *Nature (London)*, **215**, 849

91. Payne, P. R. and Wheeler, E. F. (1967). Comparative nutrition in pregnancy. *Nature (London)*, **215**, 1134

92. Benton, A. L. (1940). Mental development of prematurely born children: A critical review of the literature. *Am. J. Orthopsychiat.*, **10**, 719

93. Drillien, C. M. (1970). The small-for-date infant: Etiology and prognosis. *Pediatric Clinics of North America*, **17**, 9

94. Wiener, G. (1970) The relationship of birthweight and length of gestation to intellectual development at ages 8 to 10 years. *J. Pediatr.*, **76**, 694

95. McDonald, A. (1964). Intelligence in children of very low birth weight. *Br. J. Prev. Social Med.*, **18**, 59

96. Record, R. G., McKeown, T. and Edwards, J. H. (1970). An investigation of the difference in measured intelligence between twins and single births. *Ann. Hum. Genet., Lond.*, **34**, 11

97. Barker, D. J. P. (1966). Low intelligence: Its relation to length of gestation and rate of foetal growth. *Br. J. Prev. Social Med.*, **20**, 58

98. Birch, H. G., Richardson, S. A., Baird, D., Horobin, G. and Illsley, R. (1970). *Mental Subnormality in the Community: A Clinical and Epidemiologic Study.* (Baltimore: Williams and Wilkins)

99. Douglas, J. W. B. (1960). 'Premature' children at primary schools. *Br. Med. J.*, **i**, 1008

100. Drillien, C. M. (1964). *The Growth and Development of the Prematurely Born Infant.* (Baltimore: Williams and Wilkins)

101. Richardson, S. A. (1976). Relationship of severe malnutrition in infancy to the intelligence of school children with differing life histories. *Pediatr. Res.*, **10**, 59

102. Stein, Z., Susser, M., Saenger, G. and Marolla, F. (1973). Nutrition and mental performance. *Science (N.Y.)*, **178**, 708

103. Stein, Z., Susser, M., Saenger, G. and Marolla, F. (1973). Intelligence test results of individuals exposed during gestation to World War II famine in the Netherlands. *T. Soc. Geneesk.*, **50**, 766

CHAPTER 4

Psychological testing in studies of malnutrition*

IRVING HURWITZ

INTRODUCTION

The use of tests to assess psychological functions owes its inception and subsequent development to a number of diverse sources. Among the most relevant early work was that of Galton[1], who, in his efforts to study inheritance in genius, sought to quantify the degree of presence or absence of skills in which a specific mental function could be identified. Galton relied on techniques of psychophysical research as reported from Leipzig by Wundt[2]. Titchener[3], in the United States, also influenced by the psychophysicists, explored the objective measurement of 'pure' psychological functions which he felt could be carried out in a truly quantitative fashion if at least two conditions could be fulfilled: first, that subjects could be trained to develop the ability to report the purely sensory characteristics of the stimulus, and secondly, that the methods used to elicit the subject's report should be capable of measurement in equal intervals of stimulation at any point on a scale of intensity.

The reports of European studies were eagerly reviewed by experimental psychologists engaged in seeking viable approaches to the measurement of psychological processes. Their goal was to bring full scientific status to this emerging field, still occupied with shaking itself free of its union with philosophy. The results of these investigations suggested that measurement might indeed have some useful application even in studying individual differences, a heretofore little known line of endeavour. In 1901, Binet and Simon undertook a commission granted them by the French Ministry of Education to explore the basis of

* Work for this report was completed with support from USPHS Research Grant MH-18332.

academic functioning in children who either performed well in a school setting or those for whom progress seemed either significantly slowed or not likely to occur at all. The gravity of the responsibility undertaken by Binet and Simon was expressed by Binet in his report to the Ministry in which he stated:

> 'A [commission] formed by the Ministry decided that no child suspected of retardation should be eliminated from the ordinary school and admitted into a special class without first being subjected to a pedagogical, medical, and psychological examination from which it could be certified that, because of the state of his intelligence, he was not able to profit in an average measure on instructions given in ordinary schools. To be a member of a special class can never be a mark of distinction, and such as do not merit it must be spared the record'[4].

Binet and Simon used psychophysical measurements as one kind of data upon which to base diagnostic conclusions and educational recommendations. Their efforts to provide statistical normative data at each age level enabled children to be rated in relation to one another rather than in terms of an absolute standard. Their approach served as a model for a wide variety of techniques subsequently developed. For Binet and Simon, intelligence, as far as criteria of validity were concerned, was the child's predicted performance in the classroom, i.e. the mental age was the datum on which the child's placement in school was based. Binet and Simon defined little in the use of their test as to the specific 'nature' of intelligence, but rather adhered to the direct and clear-cut practical goal they set for themselves, namely, the prediction of school performance.

From the pioneering work of Binet and Simon, the psychological test movement flourished and proliferated. It seemed peculiarly congenial to the intense climate of pragmatism and empiricism in psychological laboratories in the United States, particularly with the rise of 'Watsonian behaviourism' and its implication for pedagogical practices. In essence, the position adopted by many experimental approaches to measurement was that if a skill or mental function was found wanting in the child, then its level could be improved by the application of behavioural techniques often based on the Pavlovian conditioned-response model, an approach still actively utilized to this day. The growth of the intelligence testing movement is documented by a review of Buros' *Mental Measurements Yearbook*[5], where the list of individual and group tests of intelligence is extensive.

For more than half a century, the debate over the actual nature of intelligence has continued, and in certain instances has intensified around such specific questions as race, social change, early education, etc. Some view intelligence as nothing more nor less than that which is represented in the test performance itself[6], while others (Pierson[7], Guilford[8], Thurstone[9]) have created elaborate theoretical and statistical models to capture the subtlety and complexity of what intelligence is actually thought to be. It is not our intention here to weigh the merits of different theoretical approaches and their measurement instruments in order to choose one or the other as the basis for a more effective definition of intelligence, but rather to describe a number of tests commonly used in clinical practice and in a wide variety of research studies aimed at establishing what the nature of the relationship is between a particular abnormal state, in this case, undernutrition, and intellectual development.

In a lengthy review article, Latham[10] states: 'In many studies, different types of protein–calorie nutrition existed in the children involved; the age of onset and the severity of malnutrition varied; and a wide range of tests was used to assess mental functioning, psychological development or intelligence. Because of a considerable methodological difference, it is difficult to compare the results between studies or to draw conclusions about a situation in different regions of the world.' Latham's review of studies dealing with the concomitants in intellectual performance of children with protein–calorie malnutrition provides a clear illustration of the relative isolation of studies from one another, resulting in 'hindrances to general interpretation and to universal conclusions . . .' Latham's review points to the use of different tests as one form of 'methodological difference' and he identifies a number of specific scales which are applicable from infancy to adolescence and adulthood in measuring the level of intellectual competence. The tests listed are the Gesell Developmental Scales, the Kuhlman-Anderson Group Intelligence Test, the Wechsler Intelligence Scale for Children, the Merrill–Palmer Scale, the Raven Progressive Matrices, the Goodenough Draw-a-Man Test, and a number of measurement procedures that were specifically developed for use in the locality of their administration, e.g. intelligence tests used only in India or South Africa.

We will describe those standardized tests that appear to have been most commonly applied in the literature, the nature of the populations used in standardization, and their relevance or appropriateness for research. It is important to note that any tests are useful primarily to the extent that they 'ask the right questions'. This is to say that the strength and limitations of the test must be defined in terms of their value in identifying such underlying processes as perception, abstraction, discrimination, rather than simply a score. Psychologists recognize that reporting only a Full Scale IQ score on the Wechsler Intelligence Scale for Children may obscure significant degrees of scatter within a subsection, and significant discrepancies between the overall scores of the major divisions of the test itself, i.e. the Verbal and Performance scales. In addition to seeking out the pattern of contributing processes in different aspects of test performance, psychologists must be aware of the characteristics of the normative sample on which the test was standardized, the reliability of the test, i.e. the consistency of the instrument in use, and its validity, i.e. the degree to which in fact the test measures what it sets out to measure in reporting results obtained in research.

The major issues confronting psychologists in the application of intelligence tests in clinical populations are concerned with whether indices of cognitive or intellectual development are generally applicable, or are likely to appear only in occasional instances or in specific populations. Psychologists deal with the question of the degree to which development in one area is or is not independent of other areas, i.e. do some processes inhibit others, are they different aspects of a general factor, or are they expressions of more specific, discrete characteristics of mental growth? While intelligence tests differ in form and content, they operate on the basis of one of two assumptions: the first, that intelligence is somehow a multifaceted entity which can be measured by an accumulation of separate scores on varying types of subtests with such scores expressed in terms of a subject's position in a normative relation to others of similar age; or that intelligence is a singular force which is best measured by single-dimension instruments, or, if varied types of measures are used, the scores are combined into a total numerical value reflecting the degree of presence of this particular general quality. The score itself may be expressed as years and months that define the subject's mental age. A simple transformation of mental age, which expresses a ratio to chronological age, is the now familiar derivation of intelligence quotient:

$$\text{Intelligence Quotient} = \text{Mental Age}/\text{Chronological Age} \times 100$$

Scores are also expressed as percentiles, standard scores, or stanines, the latter placing an individual's level of performance on a scale of 1–9. Exceptions to the multiple subtest approach to intelligence measurement will be discussed and the assumptions governing these instruments will be briefly reviewed.

In addition to the form and content of the test, that is, single task versus multiple task, paper and pencil versus manipulatable materials, tests are usually defined as either an individually administered test or a group administered test, with different degrees of confidence placed in each, usually greater in the case of individual tests.

We shall list the tests in terms of their application at successive developmental levels, i.e. those tests which assess performance of the youngest age levels and those that have their input with increasingly older populations.

INFANT AND PRESCHOOL TESTS

GESELL DEVELOPMENTAL SCHEDULE

The Gesell Developmental Schedule[11] was developed at Yale University, and is used in assessing developmental status of children from 4 weeks to 60 months of age. The child is observed both without examiner involvement as well as while interacting with a variety of objects, e.g. a ball, a picture book, etc. In addition, a parent interview is utilized to elicit information regarding developmental progress both prior to the time of the evaluation and in current behaviour that cannot be observed directly in the test situation.

The test manual describes the modal developmental acquisitions of children in monthly units up to 12 months, and beyond this, in 3-month periods of growth. There are four specific foci of interest in the assessment: motor capacity, language behaviour, adaptive skills and social and emotional state. Scoring guidelines are provided which enable a child's performance to be judged as below age level, at age level, and accelerated within these four dimensions.

Examples of motor skills tested would be sitting, crawling, standing, walking, in which each item is pinpointed as to its temporal location in an overall score for motor activity. Language behaviour reflects the degree of word acquisition, complexity of sentence structure, and breadth of verbal behaviour displayed by the child. Adaptive behaviour involves the level of use of a variety of manipulable materials such as pellets, bottles, crayons and the ability of the child to adapt to changes in the nature of these stimuli. Emotional assessment measures the quality of affect display, its appropriateness to the situation and the response to varying intensity of social stimulation to which the child is exposed.

The total assessment of these four areas yields a developmental profile. Conclusions as to normalcy of developmental rate can be formulated with a fair degree of precision in the four categories tested. However, it is this quality of precision in pinpointing age levels—i.e. the months and years reflected in specific test behaviours—that gives the scale a certain degree of vulnerability. There does not appear to be a conceptual framework which enables one to account for variations in the time of emergence of one or more separate behaviours, as is the case, for example, with Piaget's stage-approach to early development[12]. Werner[13] has criticized the Gesell scale on the grounds that it is too outcome orientated, overly concerned with the point in time where a particular performance occurs or is expected to occur, and less with what this behaviour may mean in relation to other aspects of development.

There is a tendency to ascribe slowness or acceleration by a piecemeal aggregate of isolated behaviours. Little is offered as to the nature of developmental stages of growth. Notions of differentiation and organization expressed as a systematic context which defines the relationship between different modes of behaviour in a dynamic and developmental scheme are minimal. Gesell states that the scale is essentially a measure of the neurological progress of the child. He writes: 'The text cleaves consistently to the central problem of diagnosis. There is no elaboration of theory for its own sake . . . It presents the behaviour aspects of developmental maturity from an objective standpoint . . . It is the maturity and organization of the neuromotor system with which we are chiefly concerned. We are in fact dealing with developmental neurology.'

The Gesell scale yields a Developmental Quotient with Mental Age/ Chronological Age × 100, much in the same fashion as an intelligence quotient is derived. The scale does not deal with cultural variability in child care practice during the preschool years, and may favour the child to whom specific skills are taught by concerned or ambitious parents. Nevertheless, the test is unquestionably an established instrument for categorizing specific behaviours within a *range* of time when children in the standardization population could be expected to demonstrate these behaviours, thus providing a good general guideline as to rate of development.

An abbreviated form of the Gesell scale has been devised by Hilda Knobloch[14], which has proven very useful as a screening device in assessing degree of developmental risk in infants and toddlers. This adaptation represents a practical advantage in time of administration and less complexity of scoring.

MERRILL–PALMER SCALE

The Merrill–Palmer Scale[15] is a 93-item intelligence test covering the age range from 18 months to 6 years. The score is expressed as a mental age (from which an IQ can be calculated), a standard score, and a percentile rank. The test involves language tasks, fine and gross motor skills, visual perceptual motor performance, abstraction and concept formation, and reasoning. Unlike the Gesell Developmental Scale, the Merrill–Palmer relies little on parental reports and bases its findings entirely on direct testing of the child.

The test was originally constructed to supplement the first revision of the Stanford–Binet Scale[16], by providing a relatively larger amount of nonverbal material. In a preliminary survey, a large number of tests were reviewed; the subtests included in the final version of the scale were either selected from those already published, or designed from the usual activities of children. The most promising items were tried out on children at the Merrill–Palmer School in Illinois. Results were analysed to show which subtests had the largest number of such desirable qualities as ease of administration and scoring, appeal to the child's interests and motivation, etc. In the final selection, a scale consisting of 93 items was devised.

The technique of standardization was derived from methods suggested by Thurstone[9]. Each test was located by interpolation, if necessary, at the age when 50% of the children could pass it. All tests were then ranked and numbered in order of difficulty as they are printed on the record sheet. That order is not rigidly followed in the standard administration of the test, but serves as a guide to whether or not the child has reached the probable upper limit of performance. Final scores are, as indicated, transformed into mental age levels, and percentile ranks and standard scores are available as well. No statistical analysis of the processes needed for success in these tests was offered, although brief descriptive interpretations are given for each test in the manual.

Observations of the series leads one to conclude that it contains more manipulative and nonverbal material than the Stanford–Binet and that it measures time on task performance somewhat more accurately. Consequently, important factors for success in this test are speed and accuracy in perception of form as well as in hand and eye co-ordination. Despite the apparent emphasis on manipulable and nonverbal items in the Merrill–Palmer, the five major verbal tasks included do cover a substantial age span, with progressive levels of accurate performance defining normative standards. In this respect, then, the test does provide useful data as to language development as well as with regard to nonverbal performance. Our own studies[17] yielded results comparing Merrill–Palmer performance of malnourished and normal siblings below age 5, in which significant differences were observed in fine motor skills, while verbal behaviour did not discriminate the two populations. A correlation coefficient between scores on the Stanford–Binet and the Merrill–Palmer is reported at ± 0.973, and the correlation coefficient between chronological age and Merrill–Palmer test scores was above ± 0.90.

SCHOOL-AGE LEVEL TESTS

BINET-TYPE SCALES

The Binet–Simon test has undergone four revisions since its original development in France in the early part of the twentieth century. These were published in 1916, 1937, 1964 and 1972 by Terman and Merrill[16]. The psychophysical measures were eliminated and the tasks remaining are assumed to be direct measures of independent, native (i.e. separate from the effect of experience) intellectual competence.

In the 1916 and 1937 revisions, two alternate forms of the test (L and M) were developed, so that retesting was possible within a short span of time without duplication of items. In the 1964 revision, form L-M was developed which combined both tests on the assumption that the re-testing would not occur at an interval so brief as to develop a practice effect, while at the same time providing a broad range of measurement in the items in the combined form.

The test is an age scale with statistical procedures used to determine the appropriateness of inclusion of items. Children do not receive the same tests at different age levels. There are no *a priori* considerations as to the character of basic processes involved in particular tests that were used, though item analyses have subsequently been carried out. An examination of the scale shows a wide spectrum of items tapping verbal skills, perceptual functioning, verbal problem solving, short-term memory, mathematical reasoning, eye–hand co-ordination, and perceptual motor behaviour. The Binet scale was not designed in the absence of theoretical orientation. Terman and Merrill[16] emphasized that 'direction, adaptation, and self-criticism . . . are the aspects of behaviour that can be characterized as intelligence in action'.

The Stanford–Binet was the most widely administered individual measure of intelligence for decades both in clinical settings as well as in a large number of research studies over the past 20 years. Criticism of the Binet has recently grown, particularly around lowered scores in results of testing of minority groups which led to the conclusion that these populations were generally of lesser competence. Biological ex-planations were advanced as the basis of these consistently lower scores. An alternate rationale for these findings, which many have found repugnant, has been that the Binet, which includes a greater representa-tion of verbal than nonverbal items, penalizes populations with less conventional patterns of verbal communication. In the 1960s, standard-ization of the test was carried out with populations specifically including minority ethnic groups. The somewhat surprising lack of utilization of the test in clinical research is in part due to the emphasis on verbal tasks, the lack of cross-cultural norms and the diversity of tasks at different age levels which made only overall MA data useful.

The Wechsler Intelligence Scales include the Wechsler Preschool and Primary Scale of Intelligence (WPPSI), the Wechsler Intelligence Scale for Children (WISC), the Wechsler–Bellevue Scale and the Wechsler Adult Intelligence Scale (WAIS)[18]. Wechsler's concept of intelligence is that of an undifferentiable global capacity, a 'g' factor, which enables the individual to 'act purposefully, to think rationally, and to deal effectively with the environment'. WISC derived IQs are interpreted as an index of the child's capacity to display that global ability when performance is compared with other children in the same age range. Wechsler used items which represent different types of performance rather than different items grouped by chronological age. Thus the major divisions of the test are designed to assess verbal and nonverbal performance, and within these two broad categories are a variety of subtests, six verbal and five nonverbal or 'performance' tasks. All subjects receive the same subtests.

The Wechsler Intelligence Scale for Children was standardized to 5 years of age and with publication of the WPPSI in 1969, the scale was extended down to 3 years of age. In 1974, the WISC was revised and new norms, again including a more representative sample of heterogeneous social and ethnic groups, known as the WISC-R, were published[18]. While Wechlser did not emphasize any factor or task analysis of his 11 subtests, Rapaport and Shafer[19], in their volumes on diagnostic psychological testing, did analyse the Wechsler–Bellevue subtests in terms of underlying processes. Their analysis assigned a specific dimension of function to each of the subtests in the Wechsler–Bellevue, and inasmuch as the WISC subtests are thought to be isomorphic with the Wechsler Adult Intelligence Scale, these interpretative formulations have been widely applied to the meaning of scores on the children's version. For example, the Information subtest was defined as a measure of sensitivity to and the ability to store factual detail. Similarities was classified as a measure of abstraction and conceptual skills. Digit Span was identified as a measure of attentional focus. On the Performance scale, Block Design was assumed to measure visual and spatial analysis and synthesis, while Object Assembly represented visual part–whole awareness and fine motor skill. Schafer and Rapaport sought to integrate the different subtests as representing a series of windows through which it was possible to observe one process at work either singly or in interaction with others. The end product of such observations was the integration of a whole greater than the sum of its parts and identified as 'intelligence'.

Such an attempt at defining underlying processes in the subtests of the Wechsler scales has gone beyond the intuitive notions of Rapaport and Shafer. Factor analytic studies of the WISC have revealed clusters of subtests which seem to represent identifiable cognitive dimensions. Broverman and his colleagues[20] have reported that object assembly, block design and picture arrangement represent a cognitive style defined as perceptual restructuring related to spatial ability; vocabulary, digit span and digit symbol reflect the automatization mode, i.e. the capacity of a subject to perform routine over-learned repetitive tasks swiftly and accurately. Studies by Cohen[40] and others have identified a perceptual organization factor on the WISC which includes the block design and object assembly, and a verbal comprehension factor which includes information, comprehension, similarities and vocabulary, and a freedom from distractability factor represented by the digit span. These factors led to predictions about WISC performance in populations having a clinical basis for selection. For example, studies are reported by Schafer[21], Money and Granoff[22] on endocrine and chromosomal abnormal groups, which describe differences in performance on this particular group of subtests.

A review of Buros' *Mental Measurements Yearbook* reveals that the issue of relative value of the Stanford–Binet or the Wechsler scales varies with the different purposes of each test. Commenting on this issue, Teague[23] quotes Horrock's statement: 'In general, the WISC is a convenient and intrinsically interesting test for children who are neither particularly bright nor particularly dull . . . for children who are very young or at the extreme range of intelligence, the Stanford–Binet seems to be a more adequate instrument.'

SINGLE TASK TESTS

Single task measures of intelligence, unlike the WISC and the Binet, which approach intelligence in terms of measuring multiple function as dimensions of some overall global competence, also postulate a holistic structure to intelligence. These tests approach the task of measurement by a single behaviour which, on *a priori* grounds, is thought to embody the expression of general intelligence. Two such tests are commonly encountered in the literature reporting studies of the relationship of malnutrition to intellectual development[10]; these are the Raven Progressive Matrices and the Goodenough Draw-a-Man Test.

RAVEN PROGRESSIVE MATRICES

The Raven Matrices[24] consist of a series of designs or patterns presented with a segment removed, i.e. a blank space in the test stimulus. The subject must choose which of six pieces, all of the correct size and shape, but with different internal patterns, would complete the larger test figure. Two forms of the test are in use, one for ages 5–8 consisting of three series of 12 plates in colour, and the 60-item test of black and white figures for older populations including adolescents. Since the subject is asked only to point to the correct solution, this test is widely used in assessing intelligence where less reliance needs to be placed on language skills. An examination of strategies for solving the Raven task reveals that the rule or principle which solves each item can be formulated either in verbal terms, or can be derived from the purely visual perceptual discovery of the internal structure of the stimulus.

In an unpublished study at The Children's Hospital Medical Center in Boston, Massachusetts, Dr Marion Walter found that these strategies did not appear to be related to other measures of intelligence in a clinical population of learning disabled children, but rather seemed to represent variations in cognitive style in which separate visual perceptual and verbal conceptual approaches could be demonstrated. Keir[40], in a study in Great Britain, reported that factor analysis of a large number of tests administered to British school children yield results identifying a strong spatial factor which showed significant loading on the Raven Progressive Matrices. Our own studies[25] found that a comparison between delinquent, learning problem and normal boys on a variety of temporal and spatial tasks produced differences on the former measures between clinical and nonclinical groups, but no differences on the spatial measures which included the Raven Progressive Matrices.

GOODENOUGH DRAW-A-MAN TEST

The second test of a single task type is the Goodenough Draw-a-Man Test[26] and its recent modification, the Goodenough–Harris Test[36], which adds the figure of the woman and provides more recent scoring norms. Goodenough concluded from her own observations and from a thorough study of others' research that children's drawings could be used as an indication of intellectual development. She devised a test in which children draw a man from memory. The instructions ask the child to draw the very best picture of a man the child can produce. A man was chosen by Goodenough as a standard subject for the drawings, because it is one with which all children are familiar, thus having a broader appeal; and the clothing of a male figure tends to be more uniform than that of a woman or child. Points used for scoring were chosen because they showed either a regular increase in the percentage of children succeeding at successive ages, and a clear differentiation between the performance of children who are at the same age but different school grades.

The main use of the test is a preliminary classification of intelligence. The manual itself, however, contains material for more complex psychological analyses of the children's drawings. Goodenough states: 'Drawings of children are primarily a language, a form of expression, rather than a means of creating beauty.' What the child conveys in the drawing is a complex distillate of perceptual, language and conceptual abilities. The Goodenough appears now to have been assigned a more supplementary role rather than being viewed as a reliable sole index of a child's intellectual competence. Inherent in the use of the test is the possibility that intra-individual factors reflecting motivation and emotional processes can influence the complexity of a human figure drawing. Indeed, human figure drawings are commonly used in so-called projective testing, so that certain patterns in the drawing may make it difficult to sort out the connotative from the cognitive processes involved. However, the main asset of the Goodenough appears to be the relative freedom from dependence on verbal communication involved in the task itself. The scoring reflects not only the content of the drawing, i.e. the body parts, clothing, etc. but also the degree of fine motor control evident in the use of the pencil, awareness of perspective, use of space, all of which may in fact be useful indices of cognitive growth at least in the area of fine motor skill.

In summarizing intelligence measures described to this point, it is clear that the instruments available, as well as the theoretical formulations regarding the nature of intelligence, are far from fulfilling the requirements for broad generalization in much behavioural and psychological research, including those investigations which deal with the relationship between undernutrition and psychological behaviour. Commenting on studies of psychological functioning in malnourished populations using test data, Tizard[41] stated: 'The definition of an adequate psychological test . . . constantly arises in work with children who differ from the samples of North America, British or other European populations that have been used to standardize most of our tests. The validity of individual items and subscales in measuring mental functions is almost universally low, even when the validity of scales made up of a number of items is very high.' Tizard then goes on to support the usefulness of multiple test batteries from which 'indicators of high reliability and evident face validity' could be derived.

Psychologists, of course, are concerned with the predictive implications of intelligence test scores regardless of the test from which they are derived. Two primary reasons why such importance has been attached to the notion of constancy of intelligence in subjects tested at various ages focus on the notion that an intelligence quotient represents a measure of a fixed native ability. Any significant positive correlations obtained between IQs separated in time is taken for evidence that the IQs indicate native ability, though this conclusion is justified only if environment has been held rigidly constant. In normal society enormous differences in motivation or opportunity to develop are sometimes apparent even within members of the same social group or in the same family. A second reason for attaching great importance to the findings of fairly constant IQs is the desire for practical predictions. In order to allow accurate predictions which would generate the application of programmes over a period of time, an individual's IQ must be nearly the same from year to year, or, at least, determined to vary in some regular and consistent fashion. Although a large number of studies have been carried out in attempts to determine how constant IQs actually are in groups of subjects over various time intervals, these studies are as yet inconclusive both because of difficulties in accurate measurement and because of obstacles involved in studying the same children over long periods of time in a constant environment.

SPECIFIC FUNCTION TESTS

Interest has turned recently to the use of tests for specific functions in children suffering from undernutrition when compared with performance of non-malnourished populations. Such tests are usually not normative, that is, they have not been developed to measure population performance on a standardized basis, but rather are useful in contrasting the behaviour of criterion groups in experimental and control research designs. These tests may originate in theoretical formulations regarding measurement of normal development in a particular area which are then extrapolated for use in clinical research.

An example of this approach is the investigation of Birch and his colleagues[27] in their studies of the relationship between cross-modal performance, that is, visual to auditory, auditory to visual, and reading skills in school-aged children. Such measures are described as 'intersensory' or 'neuro-integrative' and are designed to compare ability to discriminate and respond to stimuli in a different modality than that which characterizes the original stimulus. The subject may be asked to choose a visual display of dots which corresponds to a sequence of sounds, or vice versa. Findings reported in the literature[28] indicate that children with a documented history of undernutrition perform less well on these intersensory tasks than sibling controls. However, other studies utilizing this technique have suggested that the lower performance of children with reading problems is not a consequence of ineffective cross-modal or intersensory transfer but may reflect a deficit in abstraction and concept formation[29]. The explanations offered for these differences is that normal readers develop a linguistic formula for grouping the sounds or visual dot patterns which then serve as the internalized reference source for the response. Thus poor intersensory performance may really imply a language deficit and the differences between such groups as undernourished and non-malnourished populations would need to be interpreted as conceptual rather than perceptual in nature.

Wolff at The Children's Hospital Medical Center in Boston has developed an experimental technique useful in studying intersensory functioning. Cross-modal behaviour is tested by requiring judgements of same or different in comparing *sequences* of sounds and *sequences* of lights, thus isolating visual from auditory without the contaminating influence of spatial versus temporal. This method has yet to be used in clinical populations, but its application may clarify further the nature of intersensory competence in clinical and normal populations more completely than have previous techniques.

Temporal and spatial skills are obviously significant issues in development, and research in this area will certainly extend our understanding of the role of differential vulnerability (both psychologically and biologically) in these cognitive dimensions. In research on undernutrition, a careful analysis of temporal sequencing on the one hand (in both the visual and auditory modalities), and spatial organization on the other, can be crucial in determining what the critical points of developmental deficit may be.

An additional area of interest in assessing specific areas of performance in subjects with malnutrition focuses on motor development. The Lincoln–Oseretsky Test of Motor Development[30] is a technique for surveying a broad range of gross and fine motor activity. As standardized by Sloan in 1955, the test is a 36-item scale taking approximately one hour to administer (a short form has been used by Rutter[42] and others in epidemiological studies in Great Britain). Grouping of items has been carried out on the basis of their underlying motor skill, such as balance, rhythm, grasp release, lateral differentiation, and eye-hand coordination. This test is particularly useful in examining sex differences in motor skill, since norms are reported separately for females and males. In addition, tables of age level performance are published for each item, giving the percentage of subjects passing this item at successive ages, and thus enabling an examiner to place a subject's response at the corresponding chronological age.

Tests of visual perceptual motor performance are numerous in psychological testing practice. These generally fall into one of three types: (a) paper and pencil design-copying tasks as illustrated by the

Bender Gestalt Test[31] or the Beery–Buktenica Visual Motor Integration Test[32]; the Bender Gestalt Test has been carefully reviewed and scored at age levels by Koppitz[33] which permits one not only to judge the competence of the child, but also to detail the qualitative nature of the errors made; (b) paper and pencil drawings of designs from memory, e.g. the Benton Visual Retention Test[34], involving 10-second delays before drawing, or the Graham–Kendall Memory for Designs Test[35] which involves a 5-second delay; (c) reproducing geometric figures and patterns of blocks, etc. as on the Wechsler Block Design and the Kohs Block Test[43].

Other measures of visual perceptual and visual perceptual motor activities (for example, formboards, the Frostig Test of Visual-Perceptual Development[44], Porteous Mazes[37], etc.) are more detailed and time-consuming in their administration, and are less likely to be found in research designs unless their particular area of function is the central focus of the study.

SOCIAL–EMOTIONAL TESTS

The measurement of social–emotional factors in development has been approached through the use of standardized questionnaires or inter-views, both structured and open-ended, and direct observations. Open-ended interviews and observations are generally specific to the research study in which they appear, and thus need to be individually evaluated as to their applicability in other populations.

The most widely used scale of social development is the Vineland Social Maturity Scale[38], developed by Edgar Doll. This test is based on the assumption that intellectual deficits can be measured by assessing the rate of emergence of social–adaptive behaviour. The test is ad-ministered as a semi-structured interview questionnaire to the parents, allowing the examiner to pursue specific items either by more directed inquiry or by inviting the respondent to elaborate associatively to a particular response. The test is designed as an age scale similar in concept to the Binet scales, and covers the span from birth to adult-hood. In describing the Vineland, Teague[23] states: 'It provides the status of social growth or change in a child, extreme deviations from expected behaviour of a child, and the qualitative index of variation and development of abnormal populations and the index of deterioration in conditions where the child has regressed socially because of mental or physical disease and the measure of improvement following special therapy . . .'

SUMMARY

Several points warrant comment with respect to psychological test data and their use in research. The obvious cautionary principles deserve repetition in order that clarity of purpose in both test use and interpretation of test results can be obtained. Cross-cultural implications of test performance, in comparisons of subjects, and in item analyses are often ignored or de-emphasized in the use of psychological test data. Urban children in areas characterized as poverty-ridden inner city environments may interpret the same question as having a different meaning from children who are middle-class city dwellers.

This fundamental problem has ramifications for the usefulness of norms, their applicability to findings from one population to another, long-term predictions of future behaviour, and even the formulation of remedial programmes prescribed on the basis of lowered test performance in clinical populations. Control groups of either siblings or matched non-siblings drawn from the child's general community can diminish the effects of culturally disparate tasks in defining deficits in the index population. Such research designs are clearly more useful than those in which the normative data of the original test sample represent the standard of comparison for judging the effects of such circumstances as undernutrition.

Use of test results obtained in the infant and preschool period as predictors of long-term performance is a highly hazardous one. Studies reported by Kagan[39] on Central American children of preschool age and at elementary levels strongly suggest that while in the former group, marked deficits in cognitive performance involving visual perceptual motor skills, breadth of language activities, and problem solving capacity do occur, these are not evident at about age 10 or 11. Although these results do not represent longitudinal studies of individual children, they highlight the need for caution in making long-term predictions and formulations based on test results.

The issue of prediction has been heatedly debated since the publication of Jensen's critique[45] of preschool enrichment programmes and his assertions regarding the weak influence of such environmental stimulation on later IQs. Among the points stressed by Jensen was the notion of relative biological fixity of intellectual endowment and an expected failure of environmental stimulation to facilitate improvement in the level of expected competence in school. Hernstein's[6] expansion of Jensen's position, though purportedly without the latter's conclusions about the racial distribution of IQ, suggested an explanation of social and economic stratification in the United States based on tested intelligence levels and the significant correlations of parent and child scores.

We would like to underscore Latham's statement that 'previously malnourished children, while ill and in the period of time after recovery, do have below average scores on intelligence tests. The relative consistency of results does appear to prove the hypothesis that early severe malnutrition is associated with subsequent poorer scores on intelligence tests . . . However, many authors go beyond this and imply that their research shows that malnutrition *causes* a retardation of intellectual development. The data do not seem to support this conclusion of cause and effect.'

We strongly concur with this statement and would only add that the uncertainty which currently exists over the definition of intelligence, the meaning of test scores and their efficiency either in measuring 'true ability' or performance as a function of environmental stimulation, or both, should enforce in the minds of investigators who use intelligence scores in measuring the effects of undernutrition, vigorous caution and circumspection in the interpretation of such results.

REFERENCES

1. Galton, F. (1892). *Hereditary Genius* (New York: Macmillan)
2. Wundt, W. (1880). *Grundzuge der Physiolischer Psychologie*, 426. (Leipzig: Engelmann)
3. Titchener, E. B. (1905). *Experimental Psychology* (Ithaca: Cornell University Press)
4. Binet, A. (1900). Attention et adaptation. *L'Année Psychologique*, **6**, 248
5. Buros, O. K. (1959). *Mental Measurements Yearbook*, 1292. (Highland Park: Gryphon)

6. Hernstein, A. (1971). IQ: A critical survey. *Atlantic Monthly*, September, 1

7. Pierson, J. (1925). *Early Conceptions and Tests of Intelligence*, 298. (Yonkers: World Book)

8. Guilford, J. P. (1936). *Psychometric Methods* (New York: McGraw-Hill)

9. Thurstone, L. L. (1935). *Vectors of the Mind: Multiple Factor Analysis for the Isolation of Primary Traits*, 286. (Chicago: University of Chicago Press)

10. Latham, M. (1974). Protein calorie malnutrition in children and its relation to psychological development and behaviour. *Psychol. Rev.*, 54, 541

11. Gesell, A. and Amatruda, C. S. (1962). *Developmental Diagnosis*, 496. (New York: Hoeber)

12. Piaget, J. P. (1929). *The Child's Conception of the World*, 328. (New York: Harcourt-Brace)

13. Werner, H. (1954). *Comparative Psychology of Mental Development*, 354. (New York: International Universities Press)

14. Knobloch, H. (1969). *Short Form Developmental Scale*, 110. (Albany: University of Albany Press)

15. Stutsman, R. (1931). *Mental Measurement of Preschool Children*, 368. (Yonkers: World Book)

16. Terman, L. M. and Merrill, M. (1962). *Stanford-Binet Intelligence Scale*, 363. (Boston: Houghton-Mifflin)

17. Hurwitz, I., Wolff, P. H., Parikh, B., Lloyd-Still, J. and Shwachman, H. (1975). An item analysis of psychological test performance in malnourished and normal children (in preparation)

18. Wechsler, D. (1958). *The Measurement and Appraisal of Adult Intelligence*, 364. (Baltimore: Williams and Wilkins)

19. Rapaport, D. and Shafer, R. (1947). *Diagnostic Psychological Testing*, Vol. I, 465. (New York: International Universities Press)

20. Broverman, D. (1960). Dimensions of cognitive style. *J. Person.*, 28, 167

21. Shaffer, J. W. (1962). A specific cognitive defect observed in gonadal aplasia. *J. Clin. Psychol.*, 18, 403

22. Money, J. and Granoff, D. (1965). IQ and the somatic stigmata of Turner's syndrome. *Am. J. Ment. Defic.*, 70, 69

23. Poser, J. (Ed.) (1969). *Mental Retardation*, 320, (New York: Hoeber)

24. Raven, J. (1956). *Progressive Matrices*, 121. (London: Lewis)

25. Hurwitz, I., Bibace, R., Wolff, P. H. and Rowbotham, B. M. (1972). Neuropsychological function of normal boys, delinquent boys, and boys with learning problems. *Percept. Mot. Skills*, 35, 387

26. Goodenough, F. L. (1926). *Measurement of Intelligence by Drawings*, 177. (Yonkers: World Book)

27. Birch, H. G. and Lefford, A. (1963). Intersensory development in children. *Monog. Soc. Res. Child Devel.*, 28, 1

28. Birch, H. G. and Belmont, L. (1964). Auditory-visual integration in normal and retarded readers. *Am. J. Orthopsychiat.*, 44, 852

29. Blank, M. and Bridger, B. (1968). Intersensory transfer in reading disabilities. *Ann. J. Orthopsychiat.*, **9**, 103

30. Sloan, W. F. (1955). The Lincoln-Oseretsky motor development scale. *Genet. Psychol. Monog.*, **51**, 183

31. Bender, L. (1938). *Visual Motor Gestalt Test*, 184. (New York: American Orthopsychiatric Association)

32. Beery, K. and Buktenica, N. (1967). *Developmental Test of Visual Motor Integration*, 162. (Chicago: Educational Testing Bureau)

33. Koppitz, E. M. (1964). *The Bender Test for Young Children*, 195. (New York: Grune and Stratton)

34. Benton, A. (1955). *Visual Retention Test*, 108. (New York: Psychological Corporation)

35. Graham, F. and Kendall, B. (1960). *Memory for Designs Test*, 114. (Missoula: Psychological Test Specialists)

36. Harris, J. (1957). *Harris-Goodenough Draw-a-Man Test*, 226. (Boston: Riverside)

37. Porteous, S. (1955). *Porteous Maze Tests*, 320. (Palo Alto: Pacific)

38. Doll, E. (1965). *Vineland Social Maturity Scale*, 104. (Circle Pines: American Guidance Service)

39. Kagan, J. (1974). Recovery effects in culturally disadvantaged children. *Am. J. Orthopsychiat.*, **44**, 122

40. McFarlane-Smith, I. (1964). *Spatial Abilities*, 286. (London: Heinemann)

41. Tizard, J. (1972). Nutrition, public health, and education. In *Nutrition, Nervous System, and Behavior* (Washington: World Health Organization)

42. Rutter, M., Graham, P. and Yule, W. (1970). *A Neuropsychiatric Study in Childhood*, 272 (Philadelphia: Lippincott)

43. Kohs, S. (1926). *Block Test: Spatial Skills*, 165. (New York: Grune and Stratton)

44. Frostig, M. (1966). *Development Test of Visual Perception*, 40 (Palo Alto: Consulting Psychologists Press)

45. Jensen, A. (1969). Compensatory education: Success or failure. *Harv. Educ. Rev.*, **18**, 28

CHAPTER 5

Clinical studies on the effects of malnutrition during infancy on subsequent physical and intellectual development

JOHN D. LLOYD-STILL

HISTORICAL

The clinical features of nutritional marasmus have been recognized for thousands of years, for starvation has frequently directed the course of man's history. Nutritional marasmus may affect people of any age. The main features include lethargy, irritability, loss of subcutaneous fat with gross muscle wasting, a wizened face, protruding ribs and knees and feet that appear disproportionately large on the thin legs. By contrast, the syndrome which we now call kwashiorkor has been recognized only relatively recently as a nutritional disease. References to some of the earlier descriptions of kwashiorkor are given in the monograph by Trowell et al.[1] However, it was C. D. Williams, a pediatrician working on the Gold Coast, who published in 1933 the first comprehensive account in the English literature of a disease with an age of onset of 1–3 years which was always fatal unless treated.[2] Kwashiorkor means the disease of the disposed baby when the next one is born[3]. In the Ga language *kwashi* means first and *orkor* second[1].

During the next 20 years kwashiorkor was recognized and described in many countries of the world including all parts of Africa, India, Ceylon, Burma, Thailand, Malaya, Indonesia, Mexico, the Carribbean, Central, South and North America. Protein malnutrition has appeared in Europe, especially in Hungary, Italy and Greece after the 1939–1945 war. In 1949 kwashiorkor was discussed at a joint FAO–WHO expert committee meeting in Geneva. This resulted in the publication of WHO Monograph No. 8, 'Kwashiorkor in Africa' by Brock and Autret[4]. In

1954 Trowell, Davies and Dean published their book *Kwashiorkor* containing 640 references[1]. Other excellent reviews from different parts of the world are those of Waterlow in 1948 from the West Indies[5], Oomen 1953 in Indonesia[6], Gopalan *et al.* 1955 from India[7], and Gomez *et al.* 1955 from Mexico[8].

By the 1950s malnutrition was acknowledged as a disease of world-wide incidence with basically the same characteristics in all countries and with regional variations of only secondary import[9]. Pediatricians began to realize, however, that many malnourished children could not be categorized exactly into either cases of kwashiorkor or nutritional marasmus but showed clinical signs of both types of malnutrition. The term *protein-calorie malnutrition* was introduced to describe the complete spectrum of clinical conditions ranging from classical kwashiorkor to marasmus. Although most children exhibit signs of both primary protein malnutrition and total caloric undernutrition, the two distinct syndromes do exist. By *kwashiorkor* we mean the clinical condition of the sugar baby and similar cases of malnutrition. *Marasmus* is the syndrome which develops in chronically starved children who have been neglected or abandoned.

Closely related to the problem of malnutrition is the associated infection that is so commonly found in these children. The combination of malnutrition and infection is the major cause of the high infant mortality rates recorded in parts of Africa and South America. Scrimshaw *et al.*[10] believe that most cases of kwashiorkor are the result of synergism between infection and protein malnutrition. Moreover this interrelationship between infection and malnutrition may affect not only nutritional needs and metabolic equilibria but also resistance to infection and disease. Waterlow *et al.*[11] stated that one reason for the delay in getting nutritional scientists interested in studying protein–calorie malnutrition was the complicating factor caused by infections. Only when the parasitic and infective agents have been controlled or understood can the subject of dietary deficiency be recognized as worthy of study in its own right.

Another factor limiting the study of malnourished children was the association between malnutrition, ignorance, poverty and social class. Because of poverty the infant is starved and because of ignorance even that which is given is of the wrong type. Bad housing, overcrowding and poor sanitation expose the infant to infection while the mother may be forced to work for economic reasons, thus possibly resulting in neglect. Not surprisingly most of the early observations on the effects of malnutrition on the intellectual development of these children were thought to be the result of socio–economic deprivation.

Geber and Dean[12] stressed the apathy of babies with kwashiorkor and regarded the misery as more constant than any of the other physical signs. Psychological changes in pediatric disorders characterized by malnutrition without socio–economic deprivation have been described many times in the past. In the Lumlean lectures on celiac disease in 1918 Sir Frederick Still specifically referred to the psychological status of these malnourished children[13]. 'The mental capacity of these children does not seem to be affected. They remain capable of as much development ultimately as other children, but in the meantime they show rather the mental development which is normal for a child of their size than that which is normal for a child of their age. Whilst, however, the intelligence is quite good in these children they often show a curious slowness in response, as if they weighed one's question carefully before replying. I have thought that this was most noticeable when with much wasting there was marked pallor, and it seems reasonable to suppose that such *a condition must exercise some effect upon the brain* as upon other tissues. As a result of the general weakness the child is usually very quiet and apathetic, taking but a languid interest in toys and picture books. With improvement in the stools, however, the child soon begins to take more interest, though for a long time, even for some years in certain cases, it is quieter and less vigorous in its movements than a healthy child.'

During the early 1960s increasing attention was devoted to studies of the intellectual status of malnourished infants during both the acute phase and with subsequent recovery. Much of the stimulus for these studies was the result of animal experiments. McCance and Widdowson[14] had shown that the body weights of rats undernourished during suckling never reached that of the controls in spite of subsequent unlimited food intake. Although these findings have been confirmed in most animal studies, some species differences have failed to show an effect. The extent of the undernutrition and the age or so-called 'critical period' at which the animal's brain is vulnerable are the two most important variables. Experimental studies on rats with both pre- and postnatal malnutrition have demonstrated behavioural changes[15,16] and permanent reductions in brain weight[17,18]. At the same time as the animal experiments were progressing, clinical studies in humans were undertaken in South Africa, Mexico and other parts of the world, and resulted in a large bibliography with the majority of studies showing a permanent impairment in intellectual competence in the malnourished population.

In 1967 an international conference on malnutrition, learning and behaviour was held at the Massachusetts Institute of Technology (MIT). The proceedings were published as a book edited by Scrimshaw and Gordon[19]. The editors provide a running commentary and a critical evaluation ends each part of the book. This publication is an excellent synopsis of the work in this area at that date.

Several suggestions were made at the MIT conference to try and eliminate the socio–economic problems that complicate the study of malnourished populations from developing countries. Graham[20] suggested the study of individuals from nondeprived populations in the USA, who have experienced severe malnourishment during their early years because of congenital, anatomical or metabolic disorders. Latham[21] stressed the importance of sibling studies, and suggested the study of persons whose early childhood was involved in the severe food shortages of World War II in such places as Holland or Leningrad. He also recommended the study of children who were marasmic in early life from celiac disease and similar causes. During the last 3 years limited data on studies from all of these populations have been published, and as Latham had predicted these later studies from developed countries have shown some conflicting findings to those from the developing countries[22]. These findings are discussed in detail later.

Concomitant with the studies of populations of malnourished infants who suffered their insult primarily in the *postnatal* period, has been an increased interest in the importance of *prenatal* nutrition. Advances in neonatology have led to the differentiation between the premature and the small-for-gestational-age (SGA) infant. The data from the follow-up of these infants has clearly demonstrated the increased vulnerability to intellectual handicap of the small-for-gestational-age infant[23]. The contributions of Naeye and others[24] have demonstrated that prenatal malnutrition can have a permanent effect on the pathology of the offspring at least in terms of measurable indices of body size, organ size and cellular structure that are comparable with those from animal data. Whether these changes are responsible for impaired intelligence, however, is still under investigation.

EVALUATION OF NUTRITIONAL STATUS

In order to assess the prevalence and the severity of protein–calorie malnutrition in different parts of the world and to evaluate the effectiveness of nutritional programmes for the prevention and control of such malnutrition, it is desirable to use some universally acceptable practical methods for the evaluation of protein nutritional status[25].

DIETARY ASSESSMENT

Carefully controlled studies have now defined the requirements of protein, calories and other nutrients for different physiological groups. A study of the nutritional status of preschool children in the United States 1968–1970 is an example of this method[26]. Moreover, diet surveys provide information as to the amount and nature of the dietary supplements needed to be offered to the population to correct any specific deficits.

CLINICAL SIGNS

The following clinical signs have been listed as being suggestive of protein–calorie malnutrition of early childhood[27]: edema, dyspigmentation of the hair, easy pluckability of the hair, thin sparse hair, straight hair, muscle wasting, depigmentation of the skin, psychomotor changes, moon face, hepatomegaly and flaky paint dermatosis. These clinical signs are easy to detect by specially trained observers and do not require costly laboratories. They are not constantly present, however, and depend on several factors such as the local characteristics, sequence, severity and age at onset of the malnutrition. The two severe syndromes of kwashiorkor and marasmus are easy to identify.

ANTHROPOMETRY

The 6 measurements most often undertaken in field surveys of protein–calorie malnutrition include weight, length, circumference of arms, head and chest, and the triceps skin fold. Measurements are then compared with standards of reference which may be either local or international. Unfortunately local standards taken from children attending child welfare centres frequently do not approach the genetic potential for that particular community. Although internationally available standards are criticized for being genetically inappropriate, recent evidence suggests that environmental factors (especially nutrition) are of greater significance in regard to growth than are biological genetic influences[25].

Weight

The measurements of weight for age of selected samples of children is the most practical method for the assessment of the prevalence of protein–calorie malnutrition in a community. Serial measurements will indicate precisely the time of onset and duration of growth failure. The original classification of Gomez *et al.*[28] into first, second and third degree malnutrition was based on weight for age according to the Boston standards. First degree malnutrition was characterized by a mild clinical picture with a body weight ranging from 76–90% of the theoretical average for the child's age. In second degree malnutrition the weight was 61–75% of the theoretical average for the age. Treatment becomes more complicated and frequently the patient requires hospital care. In third degree malnutrition, the nutritional reserves are practically exhausted and the maximum weight is never more than 60% of the average for the age. Treatment is complicated, expensive and requires hospitalization. The mortality varies from 30–60%. Most authorities would now include all cases with edema regardless of body weight in the third degree malnutrition group. A simple classification was proposed by the Wellcome Working Party[29]. Malnutrition was defined as a reduction in body weight below 80% of the Boston 50th percentile. This corresponds approximately to the Boston 3rd percentile. All anthropometric measurements can then be expressed in relation to 10 percentile levels below the standard. Despite its simplicity, two major disadvantages of this classification include firstly the lack of information on the duration of the malnutrition, and secondly that the results expressed in this way are not comparable for different anthropometric measurements. Thus the 3rd percentile on the Boston standards corresponds to 80% of the standard of weight for age, 85% of the arm circumference, and 90% of the length.

Height

The eighth report of the FAO–WHO Expert Committee on Nutrition[30] emphasizes the importance of measurements of height or length since the extent of height deficiency in relation to age can be regarded as a measure of the *duration* of malnutrition. Seoane and Latham[31] have shown that weight for height is an index of current nutritional status whereas height for age gives a picture of the past nutritional history. Thus (1) *acute malnutrition* would include children with normal height for age, low weight for age and low weight for height. Many cases of kwashiorkor would fit into this group. (2) *Acute on-chronic malnutrition.* This would include children with low weight for age, low height for age and low weight for height. Marasmus would fit into this grouping. (3) *Past chronic malnutrition* includes children with low weight for age, low height for age, but normal weight for height. Recovered children and nutritional dwarfs would fit into this category.

Other Measurements Independent of Precise Age

A major criticism of many studies from the developing countries is that the parents may not know the precise ages of their children. The ratio weight for height is probably the most suitable age-independent measure of protein–calorie malnutrition and is preferred to weight for head circumference. (Skeletal measurements are less affected by protein–calorie malnutrition than weight.) A normal chest–head ratio in the second to fourth years of life should be 1 or greater. In protein–calorie malnutrition the chest circumference is affected more than the head circumference so that the ratio will be below 1. Other factors, however, mitigate against this as a good ratio.

The mid-arm circumference is relatively constant in healthy, well-nourished young children during the course of the second to fifth years of life. Several recent studies have confirmed the usefulness of this measurement as a simple index of protein–calorie malnutrition.

Head circumference

Until recent years, head circumference has been a rather neglected anthropometric measurement in malnourished children. This may have been related to the delay in investigating the effects of malnutrition on intelligence. Another factor is that measuring the head circumference accurately is more difficult than weight or height and there may be wide variability in the actual performance of this measurement. Nellhaus[32] could find no significant racial, national or geographical differences in head circumference after analysing reports in the world literature published since 1948. Some studies have suggested that accelerated body growth has occurred in recent years, a fact ascribed chiefly to improved nutrition in childhood and other social and sanitary measures[33]. Nellhaus found that head growth did not appear to have been affected by this, as the head circumference measurements obtained before World War II were virtually identical with the present ones.

O'Connell *et al.*[34] reported on 134 non-institutionalized children 1–15 years of age who had head circumferences below minus 2 standard deviations and found all but one to be mentally subnormal. They also found that the head circumference of 31 children with growth failure and normal intelligence was normal for age and sex, thus disproving the concept that the abnormally small child has a proportionately small head. There is a good correlation between head circumference and brain weight[35]. While 90% of the head circumference is achieved by the age of two years, however, only about 70% of the adult brain weight is achieved at this age. Dobbing and Sands[36] have described the quantitative growth and development of the human brain. They showed that the human brain growth spurt begins in midpregnancy and continues well into the second postnatal year and beyond. At least $\frac{5}{6}$ of the human brain growth spurt is postnatal. They also showed that the human brain revealed another miniature growth spurt between 12 and 18 weeks of gestation that may represent the period of neuronal multiplication. Insults to the fetus operating at this time that could specifically interfere with neuronal multiplication would include irradiation, viral infections, chromosomal abnormalities, other congenital anomalies associated with early fetal growth retardation, maternal hyperphenylalaninaemia, certain maternal medications and other unknown antecedents to mental retardation. The cytomegalovirus is the commonest known microbiological cause of brain damage in infancy[37].

It is obvious that methods which would permit an *in vivo* appreciation of the status of the human brain are of special relevance. Head circumference is an indirect measure of brain volume and has been shown to be an unreliable guide to brain composition in experimental animal undernutrition. The technique of transillumination may indicate the presence of excess fluid in the head. Another non-invasive technique is echo-encephalography, which determines the size of the ventricular cavities of the brain, and when used in conjunction with head circumference and transillumination provides more comprehensive information on brain volume *in vivo*. Vahlquist *et al.*[38] demonstrated a moderate but significant increase in the size of the cerebral ventricles in children with kwashiorkor examined up to 3–4 weeks after admission, whereas children with marasmus showed no deviation from the normal. Mönckeburg[39] referred to the increased transillumination that was found in malnourished infants in Chile and interpreted these findings as secondary to brain atrophy. Recent advances in our understanding of the battered child syndrome raise the possibility that some of those infants originally thought to be retarded secondary to malnutrition, could have suffered a subdural haematoma as a result of battering leading to the subsequent cerebral atrophy and small head circumference[40]. These observations are further reasons for caution in using head circumference as a measure of brain size in malnourished infants.

BIOCHEMICAL TESTS

At present there is no satisfactory biochemical test for malnutrition suitable for use in all parts of the world. The following have been suggested:

1. *Total protein and albumin*

Reduction of the serum protein and albumin levels is largely confined to children with kwashiorkor. Severe marasmus can be present with a normal total protein and albumin concentration.

2. *Fasting urinary urea-creatinine ratio*

Low ratios of urinary urea to creatinine are found in children eating small amounts of protein. Thus this is a measure of dietary rather than nutritional status.

3. *Urinary sulphur–creatinine ratio*

The basis of this test is similar to the urea–creatinine ratio, but it also reflects the dietary intake of high quality protein as indicated by those with a high sulphur content.

4. *Serum amino acid ratio*

The serum amino acid pattern is disturbed in kwashiorkor. This test is a good reflection of primary protein deficiency. Unfortunately in marasmus, where there is a total lack of calories, the test is of no positive help. Another disadvantage is that the sample of serum must be taken when fasting.

5. *Urinary hydroxyproline index*

This test depends on the fact that in nutritionally dwarfed children the excretion of hydroxyproline peptides is very low. The requirements of a 24-hour urine sample negates the usefulness of this test. Moreover, intercurrent infections such as hookworm or malaria result in high excretions of hydroxyproline.

6. *Urinary creatinine to height index*

This depends on the fact that loss of muscle in malnutrition results in a reduction of the creatinine excreted per 24 hours. Unfortunately this test assumes that the glomerular filtration rate is normal and again requires timed samples of urine.

Summary

Few of these biochemical tests are easy or practical to administer. Moreover, the wide variation of the malnutrition syndromes plus the superimposed factors of infection and parasitic infestation preclude the development of a single test for malnutrition. The development of a multiple computerized scoring system would be a major advance for the assessment of the malnutrition syndromes.

PATHOLOGICAL FINDINGS IN THE MALNOURISHED HUMAN BRAIN

The variations in body length and organ weights of infants and children have been documented[41,42]; recently the quantitative growth and development of the human brain has been more critically studied[36]. As a result of these observations of brain growth Dobbing and Sands suggested that in future studies the cerebellum should be weighed separately at autopsy. Information on the brain weight and composition of the malnourished human brain is sparse in contrast to the abundant literature on the malnourished animal brain. Brown[43,44] reviewed 1094 autopsies performed on Ugandan children from birth to 15 years between 1953–1964. The children were divided into a malnourished group as designated by the pathologists; otherwise they were put into the non-malnourished group even though many of the latter children had subclinical malnutrition at autopsy. Brown found that with each group the mean body weight of Ugandan children at autopsy was below the reference standard and was especially depressed in the malnourished group. The mean brain weights were significantly lower in the malnourished children as compared with the non-malnourished group and with the reference standard. The brain/body weight ratio was elevated in both groups of Ugandan children and suggested that the body weight was more depressed than the brain weight. Naeye[45] studied organ and cellular development in congenital heart disease and in alimentary malnutrition. Most of the organ abnormalities observed in the two groups were similar, suggesting malnutrition as a common aetiology. In both groups brain weight was almost 30% below control values. The subnormal weight and height at birth of many of the infants indicated a retarded prenatal growth pattern. Reasons for the retarded prenatal growth were unknown. Naeye[46] extended these studies by examining the autopsy findings in 220 children with congenital cardiac malformations. Infants with cardiac malformations dying between 1 month and 8 years were more retarded in growth than those dying in the perinatal period. The degree of retardation in brain growth was directly related to the degree of undernutrition as reflected in hepatic cell cytoplasmic mass. Further variables complicating any conclusions that can be made from this data include the relationship of subnormal intake of food, the hypermetabolic state commonly associated with cardiac failure and the effects of chronic tissue hypoxia.

Winick and Rosso[47] measured the brain weight, protein content, RNA and DNA content of nine infants who died of severe malnutrition in Chile. They found that the number of cells was reduced but the weight or protein per cell was unchanged. The three infants who weighed less than 2000 g at birth were the most severely affected. This data was interpreted as showing similar findings to those obtained in animal studies by demonstrating that severe early malnutrition can result in curtailment of the normal increase in brain cellularity with increase in age. There are, however, several important criticisms of this study. Complete data on the individual birth weights and gestational age was not included, and we know that at least 30% of the infants had suffered from fetal growth retardation as well as malnutrition. Moreover, if the data are plotted against weight instead of age, there is *no* reduction in DNA content in brain, and the reduction in cell number is proportional to the reduction in the weight of the children.

We have attempted to obtain some data on the effects of malnutrition on brain weight by analysing the autopsy findings in infants with cystic fibrosis who succumbed during the first year of life. Two groups could be identified—firstly, those with meconium ileus who were characterized by malnutrition from birth, and secondly, a non-meconium ileus group who may or may not present with symptoms of malnutrition soon after birth (Tables 5.1 and 5.2). The meconium ileus group was the more severely malnourished, and these results are shown in Figure 5.1 where the average weight, height, brain weight and head circumference values are compared for the two groups. These findings are comparable with Brown's data[43, 44], showing that weight was the most severely depressed anthropometric measurement in malnutrition. Figure 5.1 shows that height is less affected than weight. Another interesting observation is that the head circumference does not always correlate with the brain weight, and this subject was discussed previously. The uniqueness of this data is that more information on the gestational age (and thus intrauterine malnutrition) is documented compared with previous studies. Boyer[48] showed that the average birth weight of the infant with cystic fibrosis was 2.9 kg in contrast to a national average of 3.3 kg. Similar findings were obtained in our own group of patients[49]. Boyer hypothesized that this might be related to prenatal malnutrition, but unfortunately he gave no data on gestational age. Although our findings show results similar to those in other studies of malnourished infants' brains, it is notable that there is also documented evidence of fetal malnutrition that has to be taken into account before all these results are ascribed to the result of malnutrition. Further studies are needed to delineate the mechanism for these observations.

Table 5.1 Meconium ileus deaths under 1 year of age (cystic fibrosis patients)

Case	Age (mths)	Birth Wt. (kg)	Gest'l age (wks)	Brain Wt. (g)	Normal	%	Weight (kg)	Normal	%	Height (cm)	Normal	%	Head circ. (cm)	Normal	%
1	3	2·9	40	435	567 ±81	76·7	3·8	5·7	66·6	55	57·7 ±2·9	95·3	37·1	41 ±2·5	90·4
2	1	2·3	—	330	460 ±47	71·7	2·1	4·3	48·8	45	51·4 ±3·2	87·5	33	37·5 ±2	88·0
3	2	2·4	40	330	506 ±67	65·2	2·5	5·25	47·6	49	54 ±2·9	90·7	34·5	39·5 ±2	87·3
4	2	3·2	40	570	506 ±67	112·6	2·8	5·25	53·3	56	54 ±2·9	103·7	34	39·5 ±2	86·0
5	7	3·6	40	640	767 ±32	83·4	3·1	8·2	37·8	55·5	66·7 ±5·0	83·2	37·5	44 ±2·5	85·2
6	2	3·3	39	490	560 ±67	87·5	3·1	5·25	59·0	52	54 ±2·9	96·2	35	39·5 ±2	88·6
7	1	2·3	—	530	460 ±47	115·2				53	51·4 ±3·2	103·1	36	37·5 ±2	96·0
8	1	2·0	—	310	460 ±47	67·3	2·4	4·3	55·8	46	51·4 ±3·2	89·4	31	37·5 ±2	82·6
9	1	3·0	39	332	460 ±47	72·1	2·3	4·3	53·4	47·5	51·4 ±3·2	92·4	33	37·5 ±2	88·0
10	1	2·5	34	232	460 ±47	50·4	3·0	4·3	69·7	40	51·4 ±3·2	77·8	28	37·5 ±2	74·6
11	4	—	—	621	620 ±71	100·1				50	60·4 ±4·1	82·7	35	42·5 ±2·5	82·3
Mean		2·75				82·01			49·2			91·0			94·9

Table 5.2 Cystic fibrosis infants dying without meconium ileus

Case	Age (mths)	Birth Wt. (kg)	Gest'l age (wks)	Brain Wt. (g)	Normal	%	Weight (kg)	Normal	%	Height (cm)	Normal	%	Head circ. (cm)	Normal	%
1	5	—	—	645	746 ±91	86.5	—	5.7		57	62 ±3.1	91.9	38.5	42.5 ±2.5	90.5
2	3	3.2	40	472	567 ±81	83.2	4.2	5.7	73.6	56	57.7 ±2.9	97.0	39	40.5 ±2.5	96.2
3	3	2.9	39	555	567 ±81	97.9	4.2	5.7	73.6	55	57.7 ±2.9	95.3	39	40.5 ±2.5	96.2
4	3	—	—	585	567 ±81	103.1	4.6	5.7	80.7	60	57.7 ±2.9	104.0	38	40.5 ±2.5	93.8
5	3	3.3	40	505	567 ±81	89.1	2.9	5.7	50.8	54.5	57.7 ±2.9	94.4	37	40.5 ±2.5	91.3
6	10	2.3	40	750	850 ±96	88.2	5.4	9.4	57.4	64	69.7 ±3.9	91.8	41	46 ±3	89.1
7	3	3.2	40	450	567 ±81	79.3	3.2	5.7	56.1	57	57.7 ±2.9	98.7	35	40.5 ±2.5	91.8
8	1	3.3	40	400	460 ±47	86.9	2.9	4.3	67.4	56	51.4 ±3.2	108.9	34	37 ±3	91.8
9	1	3.3	40	430	465 ±47	92.5	3.0	4.3	69.7	52	51.4 ±3.2	101.1	—	37 ±3	
10	2	2.1	34	685	506 ±67	135.4	3.9	5.25	74.2	61	54 ±2.9	113.0	40	39 ±3	102.5
11	5	—	—	720	746 ±91	96.5	4.5	6.8	66.1	68.5	62 ±3.1	110.4	41.5	42.5 ±2.5	97.6
12	12	3.4	40	910	954 ±35	95.3	7.5	10.0	75.0	78	73.8 ±4.1	105.6	42.8	46.8 ±2.5	91.4
13	8	2.4	—	750	774 ±95	96.9	5.3	8.6	61.6	62	68.2 ±3.4	90.9	42	45 ±3	93.3
14	4	2.9	39	480	620 ±71	77.4	4.5	6.2	72.5	55	60.4 ±4.1	91.0	39	41.5 ±2.5	93.9
Mean		2.93				93.4			62.76			99.57			93.8

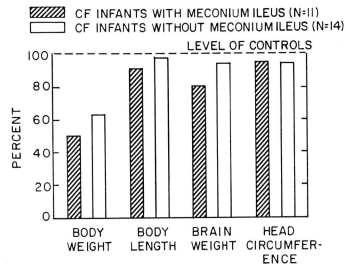

Figure 5.1 Showing percentage body weight, body length, brain weight and head circumference in 2 groups of infants dying with cystic fibrosis (with and without meconium ileus).

VARIABLES IN STUDYING MALNOURISHED POPULATIONS AND DATA FROM STUDIES 1–13 (TABLE 5.3)

SOCIO–ECONOMIC STATUS

There is evidence that children whose parents have low income, unskilled manual jobs or minimal education perform less well in school and on intelligence tests than children whose parents have a higher income, skilled technical or professional occupations and higher education levels[50]. Richardson and co-workers[51] studied children in Aberdeen and demonstrated a relationship between social class and mental ability. There was no social class trend in the prevalence of severe mental subnormality (IQ less than 50) and relatively little variability from one social class to another. By contrast in the mild to moderately mentally subnormal (IQ 50–75) the prevalence is strongly influenced by social class with clear increases at every level from upper to lower. Moreover women of an upper social class upbringing have children with higher intelligence and reading test scores than women from a lower social

Table 5.3 Comparison of findings from 13 studies of malnourished children

YEAR	1963	1965	1965	1966	1967	1968
STUDY	Stoch and Smythe	Cabak and Najdanvic	Cravioto and Robles	Cravioto *et al.*	Liang *et al.*	Mönch burg
	1	2	3	4	5	6
COUNTRY	S. Africa	Yugoslavia	Mexico	Guatemala	Indonesia	Chil
FAMILY						
SOCIAL CLASS	Low	1/3 Professional/Army	Low	Low	Low	Low
IQ PARENTS	19·6 ± 9·0 (Raven)	—	—	—	—	—
PROBLEMS	+ + + +	+	+ + +	+	—	+ +
BIRTH						
GESTATION	—	—	—	—	—	—
BIRTH WEIGHT (kg)	(3 premature)	—	—	—	—	3·3
OBSTETRIC	—	—	—	—	—	—
NEONATAL	—	—	—	—	—	—
NUMBER CHILDREN STUDIED	21	36	20	143 (Rural) 120 (Urban)	64	14
MALNUTRITION						
DEGREE	< 60%	< 60%	< 60%	< 25% Height	70%	< 60
DURATION (mos.)	—	—	—	—	—	6
GASTROENTERITIS	Yes	No	Yes	Yes	—	Yes
FIRST SEEN	10–16 mos.	4–24 mos.	< 6 mos.	6–11 yrs.	5–7 yrs.	3–11 m
CRITICAL PERIOD	< 16 mos.	< 24 mos.	< 6 mos.	—	2–4 yrs.	< 11 m
CONTROLS						
SIBLINGS OTHERS	Yes	Local Standards	N. America Standards	Upper 25% Height	Yes	Yes
UNDERNOURISHED	Yes	No	No	No	Yes	Yes
ADMISSION						
HEIGHT	< 3%	—	< 3%	—	< 3%	< 3
WEIGHT	< 3%	< 25%	< 3%	—	—	< 3
HEAD CIRCUMFERENCE	< 3%	—	—	—	—	—
FOLLOW-UP (Years)	8	7–14	1	—	5–12	3–6
AGE AT FOLLOW UP	11	7–14	1	6–11	5–12	3–6
< 5 YEARS IQ TESTS	Merrill Palmer Gesell		Gesell			Gese Bine
> 5 YEARS	Stanford Binet Wisc	Binet Simon		Birch and Lefford	WISC Good-enough	
FOLLOW UP						
HEIGHT	3%	Average	—	—	—	< 3
WEIGHT	< 3%	Average	—	—	—	25%
HEAD CIRCUMFERENCE	< 3%	—	—	—	—	< 3
IQ	Low	Low	Low	Low	Low	Low
DURATION (Days) HOSPITALIZATION	—	—	122	—	—	—

1968 'hampakan et al. 7	1970 Chase and Martin 8	1971 Birch et al. 9	1971 Hansen et al. 10	1972 Hertzig et al. 11	1974 Valman 12	1974 Lloyd-Still et al. 13
India	U.S.A.	Mexico	S. Africa	Jamaica	U.K.	U.S.A.
Low	Low	Low	Low	Low	Upper 1/3	3/5 (Hollingshead)
Illiterate	Low	—	—	—	—	108 ± 11·3 (WAIS)
+ +	+ + + +	+ + +	—	+ +	No	No
—	—	—	—	—	Normal	39 weeks
—	2·48	—	—	—	Normal	2·9
—	—	—	—	—	Normal	Normal
—	Normal	—	—	—	Normal	Normal
19	19	37	40	74	21	41
washiorkor	<60%	Kwashiorkor	Kwashiorkor	Kwashiorkor 3–24 mos.	<60%	70%
—	12	—	—		3–16 mos.	>4 mos.
—	Yes	Yes	Yes	Yes	No	No
8–36 mos.	1½–12 mos.	6–30 mos.	10–36 mos.	3–24 mos.	Birth–27 mos.	Birth–2 mos.
<36 mos.	<12 mos.	6–30 mos.	<36 mos.	<24 mos.	<27 mos.	<6 mos.
		Yes	Yes	Yes		Yes
Yes	Yes	No	No	Yes	Yes	No
Yes	No	No	Yes	Yes (Siblings)	No	No
—	<3%	—	<3%	—	—	<3%
—	<3%	—	<3%	—	—	<3%
—	—	—	—	—	—	<3%
7–10	3–4	5–14	10	5–10	3–14	2–21
8–11	3–4 Yale Rev. Dev. Exam.	5–13	10	5–10	3–14	2–21 Merrill Palmer
Birch and Lefford		WISC	WISC Goodenough	WISC	Goodenough	WISC
Average	<3%	—	<3%	—	Average	3–25%
Average	<3%	—	<3%	—	Average	3–25%
Average	<3%	—	—	—	—	12%
Low	Low	Low	Normal	Low	Normal	Low <5 yrs. Normal <5 yrs.
—	—	42	—	56	130	56

class upbringing even though social class after marriage is the same for both groups.

There is widespread evidence that a child's mental ability is influenced by the general social environment in which he is raised, the types of learning to which he is exposed, and by general life experiences. The social conditions in which learning is least conducive to optimum mental development are generally similar to those in which the poorest level of nutrition is likely to exist. In order to clearly demonstrate that malnutrition in children is the cause of mental subnormality or of a general impairment of mental ability at all levels, it is necessary to demonstrate an effect distinct from that caused by social conditions. This has not yet been done. Moreover we know that the same environments characterized by poor social and poor nutritional factors co-exist with the problems of inadequate antenatal care, poor hygiene, multiple infections such as the cytomegalovirus, and a high infant mortality rate. All these factors can directly or indirectly cause insults to the central nervous system resulting in impaired mental ability. Another important facet is that the assessment of mental ability with the exception of severe mental subnormality cannot be made with any predictive certainty until the child is 7 or 8 years old[51]. These additional factors must be accounted for and ruled out *before* the cause or role of poor nutrition in impaired mental development can be clearly established. Food contributes much more than nourishment to the individual, and it is involved in a variety of significant social interactions and stimuli[52].

Belmont and Marolla[53] studied the relation of birth order and family size to intellectual performance measured by the Raven Progressive Matrices on 400000 19-year-old males born in the Netherlands in 1944 through 1947. They found that birth order and family size had independent effects on intellectual performance. There was an inverse relationship between family size and Raven score; as family size increased the level of ability declined. The effect of family size was strongest in the manual group and less marked in the nonmanual group. In contrast to the effects of family size, the effects of birth order position on intellectual performance within each family size was relatively consistent across all social groups. So too as birth order position becomes greater the level of ability declined. First borns, excluding individuals from one-child families, consistently showed better Raven performance than

REFERENCES FOR TABLE 5.3 (STUDIES 1–13)

1. Stoch, M. B. and Smythe, P. M. (1963). Does undernutrition during infancy inhibit brain growth and subsequent intellectual development. *Arch. Dis. Childh.*, **38**, 546
   Stoch, M. B. and Smythe, P. M. (1968). Undernutrition during infancy, and subsequent brain growth and intellectual development. In *Malnutrition, Learning and Behavior*, (N. S. Scrimshaw and J. E. Gordon, editors) p. 278 (Cambridge, Massachusetts: MIT Press)

2. Cabak, V. and Najdanvic, R. (1965). Effect of undernutrition in early life on physical development. *Arch. Dis. Childh.*, **40**, 532

3. Cravioto, J. and Robles, B. (1965). Evolution of adaptive and motor behavior during rehabilitation from kwashiorkor. *Am. J. Orthopsychiat.*, **35**, 449

4. Cravioto, J., DeLicardie, E. R. and Birch, H. G. (1966). Nutrition, growth and neurointegrative development: an experimental and ecologic study. *Pediatrics*, **38**, 319

5. Liang, P. H., Hie, T. T., Jan, O. H. and Giok, L. T. (1967). Evaluation of mental development in relation to early malnutrition. *Am. J. Clin. Nutr.*, **20**, 1290

6. Mönckeberg, F. (1968). Effect of early marasmic malnutrition on subsequent physical and psychological development. In *Malnutrition, Learning and Behavior*, (N. S. Scrimshaw and J. E. Gordon editors) p. 269 (Cambridge, Massachusetts: MIT Press)

7. Champakam, S., Srikantia, S. G. and Gopalan, C. (1968). Kwashiorkor and mental development. *Am. J. Clin. Nutr.*, **21**, 844

8. Chase, H. P. and Martin, H. P. (1970). Undernutrition and child development. *N. Engl. J. Med.*, **282**, 933

9. Birch, H. G., Piñeiro, C., Alcalde, E., Toca, T. and Cravioto, J. (1971). Relation of kwashiorkor in early childhood and intelligence at school age. *Pediatr. Res.*, **5**, 579

10. Hansen, J. D. L., Freesemann, C., Moodie, A. D. and Evans, D. E. (1971). What does nutritional growth retardation imply. *Pediatrics*, **47**, 299

11. Hertzig, M. E., Birch, H. G., Richardson, S. A. and Tizard, J. (1972). Intellectual levels of school children severely malnourished during the first two years of life. *Pediatrics*, **49**, 814

12. Valman, H. B. (1974). Intelligence after malnutrition caused by neonatal resection of ileum. *Lancet*, **i**, 425

13. Lloyd-Still, J. D., Hurwitz, I., Wolff, P. H. and Shwachman, H. (1974). Intellectual development after severe malnutrition in infancy. *Pediatrics*, **54**, 306

the later born. Thus the effects of family size were not present in all social classes but the effects of birth order were consistent across social class. The studies of Stein *et al.*[54] on the effects of the Dutch famine included subjects from all social classes. These authors commented that one of the striking findings was the strong association of social class with mental performance. They found that the frequency of severe mental retardation among survivors of the birth cohorts was related neither to conception nor to birth during the famine. The frequency of mild mental retardation too was related neither to conception nor to birth during the famine.

In the thirteen studies discussed in detail only three included children from families that were not in the lower social scale. Study 2 had a third of the children coming from professional and Army backgrounds. Study 12 had most families from the top three social classes and Study 13 had an average social class of 3 out of 5. It is important to note that Studies 12 and 13 were *unable* to demonstrate intellectual impairment when the children were studied at intervals of over 5 years from the date of the nutritional insult.

PARENTAL INTELLIGENCE QUOTIENT

The controversy over whether IQ is determined by nature or nurture seems less intense than it was a decade ago[55]. Psychologists are now more interested to what degree and in what ways genetic and environmental variables influence IQ score. Bayley[56] found that the relationship between (a) parental height and child's height and (b) parental education and child's mental test score increased with age. However the pattern of correlation between parental education and the child's mental score differed from the parent/child height correlations. The correlation between parental education and child's IQ tended to be higher from maternal education than from paternal education for the preschool years. Kagen and Moss[55] investigated the Stanford Binet IQ at years 3, 6 and 10 and (a) parental education and (b) parental Otis IQ score. The results indicated that maternal education showed higher correlates than paternal education with the IQ of both boys and girls at all three ages. It was suggested that the results of these studies indicate that environmental pressures may play an important role in the determination of a child's IQ score. In contrast to Bayley's data, the Fels study[55] indicated that paternal height showed higher correlates than maternal height for the height of both boys and girls during the first 10 years of life.

The data on parental IQ was noted in only three studies. In Study 1 the Raven tables gave a range of 11–55% with a mean raw score of 19.59 ± 9.04 for the parents of the undernourished group. These are extremely low values. In Study 13 the mean IQ (WAIS) of 31 parents was 108 ± 11.3. In Study 8 the parental IQ was said to be low but no data was given. Study 11 was going to provide data in a later paper. Study 7 mentioned that most of the parents were illiterate. Thus this important information is lacking from the majority of studies reviewed.

SIBLING AND CONTROL DATA

Theoretically siblings should be the best controls in studies on malnutrition and mental development for they have all shared a common experience in exposure to the socio–economic, familial and environmental factors present. There are, however, several disadvantages to the use of siblings as controls. (1) Many of the families from the lower socio–economic populations have had different fathers for different children, and thus study of the sibling does not necessarily exclude the genetic variable. (2) Demographic data suggest that having a child hospitalized for severe malnutrition identifies the family in which all children are at risk for significant undernutrition on a chronic basis. (3) Siblings unless twins, are different in ages and ordinal position; both these factors may affect child-rearing practices as well as intellectual outcome[53]. (4) Most of the studies on siblings compare the severely malnourished child who required hospitalization to the non-hospitalized sibling control. The effects of hospitalization are discussed later. Latham[57] noted that malnutrition leading to hospitalization does not cause greater cessation of growth than does chronic malnutrition of children who have not been treated in the hospital. (5) There is always the possibility that the severely malnourished child suffered from maternal deprivation with a lack of parental stimulation resulting in delayed intellectual development.

Some of the disadvantages from the use of sibling controls could be alleviated by including a second comparison group composed of unrelated classmates or neighbours closest in age to the index child. Thus the three groups would consist of index cases, sibling controls and comparison controls. A second alternative method would be to study children with diseases such as cystic fibrosis or congenital malformations of the gastrointestinal tract that resulted in gross malnutrition, and to compare these children with their healthy sibling controls. Under these circumstances one would not be dealing with an overall population suffering from chronic undernutrition.

Four of the thirteen studies used siblings as controls (Studies 9, 10, 11 and 13). In all studies index cases were exposed to a period of hospitalization at some time compared with their non-hospitalized siblings. The number of children investigated was comparable and of adequate size with all studies ranging from 37 to 41 patients. All came from the lower socio-economic group except in Study 13. Study 9 found that the full scale WISC IQ of the index cases was 68.5, and of the controls 81.5. Verbal and performance differences were of similar magnitude and in the same direction. Study 10 could find no difference on the WISC and Goodenough Harris drawing test. Study 11 showed that full scale and verbal IQ were significantly lower in the index cases than the siblings and that all IQ measures were significantly lower in the index cases than in the comparison group. Study 13 found a significant difference on the Merrill Palmer test performed on children under the age of 5 years, but was unable to demonstrate a difference on the WISC in those children over 5 years of age.

In summary, the data from these sibling studies shows conflicting results. The limited data would indicate that the siblings in most of these studies were themselves subclinically malnourished and suffered the complicating factors of socio–economic deprivation.

PRENATAL, OBSTETRIC AND NEONATAL FACTORS

The importance of the above factors in influencing subsequent intellectual development needs no emphasis. Chapter 2 has clearly defined the ways in which these variables may cause effects on the offspring. The data discussed below demonstrates the inadequacy of this information in over 90% of the studies on malnourished infants discussed, despite the fact that many of these investigators concluded that the malnutrition alone caused the mental impairment demonstrated in their patients.

The prenatal history is absent from *all* studies reviewed. Gestational age is available in Study 12 where it was normal and Study 13 where the average gestational age was 39 weeks. Birth weight was recorded in 5 of the 13 studies. Three of the 21 children in Study 1 were premature. Studies 6, 12 and 13 showed a normal distribution for birth weight (2.9–3.33 kg). However, in Study 8 the average birth weight was only 2.48 kg. Neonatal progress was only documented in Studies 12 and 13.

CRITICAL PERIODS OF VULNERABILITY OF THE BRAIN

Dobbing and his co-workers have made several significant contributions to our understanding of the importance of the critical period of brain growth[36,58–63]. They described two critical periods of brain growth in the human, the first at 10–18 weeks gestation as a result of neuroblast multiplication and a second phase beginning in mid-gestation and continuing well into the second postnatal year and beyond. The difficulties of extrapolating data on fetal brain growth from one species to another is related to the timing of the brain growth spurt. In the rat the major brain growth spurt is postnatal, in the guinea pig prenatal, and in the pig perinatal. Although the human brain growth spurt was originally thought to resemble the pig, it is now realized that $\frac{5}{6}$ of the human brain growth spurt is postnatal and thus more closely resembles the rat.

The brain during its growth spurt is vulnerable to environmental modifications both physically and behaviourally[60]. The factors affecting the fetus at 10–18 weeks when the neuroblast multiplication is maximum include radiation, viral infections, chromosomal anomalies and drug therapy considered hazardous to neuronal division. The major brain growth spurt in the human beginning at mid-gestation and lasting for 3–4 years is accompanied by a marked increase in dendritic complexity in association with synaptic connectivity. Although we can measure reduction in glial cell number and myelination, technical difficulties have delayed the measurements of dendritic contributions. It has been suggested that the myelin content of the brain may be reduced only during the period of myelination[58].

It has been shown in the rat that the cerebellum is differentially vulnerable to nutritional growth restriction[60] resulting in increased clumsiness on specific neurological testing. Most of the animal nutritional experiments, however, have involved a degree of undernutrition much more severe than any likely to occur in the human. The human cerebellum is also characterized by a peculiarly rapid rate of growth and one would expect it to show the greatest effects of growth restriction which would be manifested by deficits in fine motor function. The data on the major brain growth spurt in the human[36] demonstrates how the full-term newborn and even more so the premature infant is especially vulnerable to nutritional deprivation. Whether interference with myelination will result in an impairment of future brain function or whether there are other systems in the brain which are more important remains to be resolved. Glial cell number and myelin lipids have been measured because they were easy to measure and for no other reason[62].

The extraordinary metabolic, neurochemical changes that accompany these events and may therefore be sensitive to growth restriction are still virtually uninvestigated because of technical difficulties. From animal experiments with rats the following lasting effects of early growth restriction have now been documented[63].

1. *Small brain size.* The cerebellum is more affected than the rest of the brain.
2. *Fewer cells* by DNA analysis; these are disproportionately fewer in the cerebellum.
3. *Less lipid,* especially in those lipids most characteristic of myelin.
4. *Altered enzyme activity.*

In summary, there is good evidence for the vulnerability of the brain during its growth spurt. We do not know and cannot yet define the physical basis within the brain of higher mental function and human achievement. Neither numbers of glial cells nor myelin were ever considered to be primarily related to intellect. Demonstrations that malnourished children's brains have too little myelin or too few glial cells are thus not likely to have been intellectually inferior because of these specific deficits[62]. In practical terms we would expect that the growth retarded baby would either have to be growth restricted for a substantial portion of the period from mid-pregnancy through about 2 postnatal years, or alternatively be severely malnourished for a shorter period.

Eleven of the 13 studies involved children whose initial episode of malnutrition occurred under 2 years of age. Five of these studies had information on the children's nutritional status between birth and the first 6 months of life. Thus the majority of investigated children were malnourished in the so-called critical postnatal period. Data on the earlier critical period of neuroblast multiplication (10–18 weeks) is extremely difficult to obtain and was absent in all studies.

DURATION OF HOSPITALIZATION

Bowlby has outlined the phases that a toddler goes through on admission to hospital[64]. The initial phase of *protest* may last from a few hours to a week or more and is indicative of separation anxiety. *Despair* succeeds protest and the behaviour of the child suggests increasing helplessness. The active physical movements diminish or come to an end and he may cry monotonously or intermittently. He is withdrawn, inactive, makes no demands on the environment and appears to be in a state of deep mourning. This is a quiet stage and sometimes is erroneously presumed to indicate a diminution of distress. Lastly there is the phase of *detachment* which sooner or later succeeds protest and despair and is often welcomed as a sign of recovery. In this phase the child may appear cheerful and unafraid of everyone. However this sociability is superficial and underneath he no longer cares for anyone. This detachment is a form of defence. Bowlby advanced the thesis that the three types of response—separation anxiety, grief and mourning, and defence—are phases of a single process and when treated as such each illumines the other two. Attachment behaviour and anxiety responses appear similar in humans and other species and the same is true of fright responses in the absence of the mother. In such circumstances the young of many species freeze. It seems almost certain that every child who has not been institutionalized develops during his first year clear preference to one person, namely the person who cares for him and whom we call 'mother'. Schaffer *et al.*[65] showed that separation anxiety on losing mother was not exhibited before about 6 months of age. It seems probable that as yet undefined influences are still present during the first 6 months but their significance is still unknown.

Cravioto and Robles[66] in an important and widely quoted paper investigated the development of children suffering from third degree malnutrition by performing Gesell psychological testing at 2 week intervals throughout hospitalization. The average period of hospitalization of the six children admitted under 6 months of age was 161 days (range of 98 to 192 days). The average period of hospitalization of the nine children admitted between 15 and 29 months was 96 days (range of 40 to 180 days). These differences in the duration of hospitalization between the two groups are significant, $p < 0.02$. As the patients recovered from malnutrition the differences between the chronological age and the developmental age in the fields of adaptive, motor, language and personal social behaviour was found to decrease except in the group of children whose chronological age on admission was below 6 months. In these the initial deficit remained constant during the entire observation period which was up to $6\frac{1}{2}$ months. These findings were interpreted as showing that the children severely malnourished during the first 6 months of life might have sustained a permanent mental deficit.

Several serious criticisms of this interpretation can be made. (1) The follow-up period was of inadequate duration for this conclusion. (2) The period of hospitalization for the two groups is significantly different ($p < 0.02$). (3) The quality of the environment in the hospital during the periods from 98 to 192 days is not stated. There is no reason to believe that this would be any different to being institutionalized in terms of its psychological effects on the child.

Only two of the studies quoted (Studies 1 and 4) investigated children who had *never* been hospitalized. The data on the other studies showed a variation in duration of hospitalization from 16 to greater than 360 days. This variable of the duration of hospitalization may be one of the more important factors accounting for the wide variation in results reported from different studies. The effects of the prolonged duration of hospitalization of malnourished children is an important variable that has been neglected.

EFFECTS OF CHRONIC DISEASE

Medical progress has improved survival rates of premature infants and children suffering from conditions with high mortality rates such as cystic fibrosis or congenital malformations of the heart and gastrointestinal tract. A large proportion of chronically ill children also have serious psychological and social problems which may be a consequence of their physical condition. The findings of three epidemiological surveys relating to the psychological and social consequences of chronic physical disorders have been described[67]. Children with chronic physical disorders were subdivided by type, duration and severity of illness, and these characteristics were related to the frequency of secondary handicaps in the areas of educational achievement, behaviour and psychological maladjustment. In each of these areas it was found that the chronically ill child fared significantly less well.

Rasoff *et al.*[68] evaluated the effect of cyanotic congenital heart disease on intelligence quotient in a 5-year study of 98 children with cyanotic and 100 with acyanotic congenital heart disease. Eighty-one normal siblings and 40 well children were also tested. Cyanotic children scored significantly below acyanotic and well children. When IQ was adjusted for physical incapacity, the difference between cardiac groups was reduced. A major finding was that incapacity is significantly related to intellectual functioning in the early years, but the correlation between Stanford–Binet IQ and incapacity beyond 3 years was slight. Silbert *et al.*[69] investigated 42 children of normal intelligence with congenital heart disease between the ages of 4 and 8 years, who were tested for general intelligence, perceptual motor function, and gross and fine motor co-ordination. Three groups of children were tested: (1) those with cyanotic heart disease; (2) those with non-cyanotic heart disease and a history of congestive heart failure; and (3) those with non-cyanotic heart disease and a benign medical history. The first group had lower IQ scores, did less well in perceptual motor tests, and had poorer gross motor co-ordination than children in the third group. Children of the second group occupied an intermediate position.

Since the indirect effects of early motor restriction might have similar consequences to those of hypoxia, the results were rearranged and statistically tested so that the effects of cyanosis could be assessed independent of the child's general activity level. No difference could be noted. It is impossible, however, to exclude other factors accounting for similar effects to the hypoxia such as secondary polycythaemia, increased blood viscosity, or local thrombosis in the cerebral vasculature.

The literature on the psycho-social aspects of cystic fibrosis (CF) has been reviewed[70], and all studies document that CF results in psycho-social consequences for patient, parents and family. The three studies[71–73] investigating the IQ show that CF children are not significantly different from normal children in regard to the distribution of IQ. Kulczycki *et al.*[73] noted the mean IQ for CF children under 3 years of age was 97, and for those over 3 years it was 110. They suggested that the test performance of the child under 3 years of age might have been depressed as a result of their illness. The sample size in these studies reviewed varied from 11 to 26 children, and generalizations based on such small numbers are subject to considerable error. The only article commenting on academic functioning[71] noted considerable educational retardation even for those children of average or above average intelligence.

According to the data available, other chronic diseases were excluded from the malnourished children investigated for intellectual functioning in Studies 1 to 11. Both Studies 12 and 13 investigated children with chronic diseases including congenital disorders of the gastrointestinal tract and cystic fibrosis. Interestingly, despite the adverse effects of chronic disease discussed previously, neither of the latter two studies could find any overall diminution in intellectual performance on prolonged follow-up. Some of the more subtle changes in fine motor functioning are described elsewhere[103].

RECOVERY FROM MALNUTRITION AND DATA FROM STUDIES 1–13 (TABLE 5.3)

PHYSICAL PARAMETERS

Height

Undernutrition reduces the rate of growth. Since bones have relatively high priorities, growth in height is interfered with less than growth in weight which results from muscular development and the accumulation of fat[74]. In pre-school children stature and skeletal maturation do not necessarily run parallel and a pathological exaggeration of these effects is the cause of dwarfs and giants[75]. Environment does not necessarily affect both equally and if growth is delayed more than maturation (as with illness or undernutrition) the size of the adult may be reduced.

The literature on the potential for recovery in height after malnutrition is controversial and further references can be obtained from the following papers. Garrow and Pike[76] followed 56 Jamaican children admitted with severe malnutrition for 2–8 years and could find no evidence that a period of severe malnutrition in infancy *per se* caused stunting of growth in these children compared with their sibling controls. Latham[57] has pointed out, however, that probably neither group in the Jamaican study had reached their full growth potential. Barr *et al.*[77] studied malnourished children with celiac disease at 1 year (± 3 months) and found that they caught up completely in weight, height and bone age during a dietary treatment of 3 years. On the other hand, celiac disease rarely presents before 6 months of age and the degree of malnutrition was frequently less severe than in some other studies. Graham *et al.*[78] followed 150 Peruvian children severely malnourished in infancy. Of this entire group eight had the benefit of a dramatic improvement in home environment and were matched with a similar control group on admission to the hospital who continued to grow at a rate below the third percentile. The eight favoured children had gains in height beginning as late as the 88th month and at the mean age of 9 years were on the 25th percentile of the same standard.

The results of follow-up measurements of height were documented in 8 out of the 13 studies. Studies 1, 6 and 8 documented a failure of catch-up in height. Study 6 had no controls. Studies 1 and 8 did not have sibling controls and in Study 8 there were marked differences in the social functioning between the two groups. Sibling controls were used in Studies 10 and 13, and in neither study could a significant difference in catch-up height be demonstrated. Moreover Studies 2, 7 and 12 were also unable to demonstrate a deficiency in catch-up height even though siblings were not used as controls. Other explanations for these equivocal results in recovery of height could be related to social class and parental IQ (the vast majority of *all* studies were from lower social classes), or related to problems in the social environment (suggestive evidence indicates that these were more severe in the Studies 1, 6 and 8 with failure in catch-up of height).

The results from the studies reviewed confirm the importance of defining the detailed criteria of the study before generalizing about conclusions leading to permanent stunting in height. Nevertheless, deficits in catch-up height occurred in nearly 50% of the reported series reviewed.

Weight

Recovery of weight loss in malnourished children may be affected by altered body composition[79], altered absorptive functioning including carbohydrate metabolism[80] and changes in endocrine function[81]. The interaction of these factors still remains poorly understood. Parra *et al.*[82] studied the changes in growth hormone, insulin and thyroxine values and on the energy metabolism of marasmic infants and suggested that the hormonal changes were a secondary adaptive mechanism which maintains muscle composition as close to normal as possible.

A malabsorptive syndrome is frequently part of the clinical picture in infantile malnutrition. Pathological findings may include intestinal and pancreatic atrophy. Viteri *et al.*[83] studied intestinal absorption of a variety of metabolites and vitamins in children with protein–calorie malnutrition on admission to hospital and at various stages during recovery. Recovery was associated with a rapid improvement in intestinal absorption for nitrogen, D-xylose and vitamin A and slower improvement in absorption of fat and vitamin B_{12} which was closely associated with the protein nutritional status of the child. The relationship between the nutritional status, alterations in intestinal microflora and improvement in absorption remains to be defined.

Differences in the recovery rate from protein–calorie malnutrition range from slow in South Africa and Chile to more rapid in Jamaica[84]. In Chile marasmus is the typical form of protein–calorie malnutrition seen and is usually complicated by gastroenteritis, whereas in Jamaica marasmic kwashiorkor predominates, occurring in the second year of life. Ashworth[85] analysed in detail the growth rate of eight children recovering from protein–calorie malnutrition in Jamaica. She showed that once a child with protein–calorie malnutrition has reached his expected weight for height, he will tend voluntarily to regulate downwards his food intake. Dietary treatment regimens were aimed at providing at least 165 calories or 3.8 g of protein per kg of body weight during the first few months of treatment. All children remained in hospital at least 3 months. In normal circumstances children with kwashiorkor and marasmus are discharged much earlier and long *before* normal weight for height has been reached. It might be very difficult for them to continue this high calorie, high protein diet at home. This may account for the fact that many of these children never reach normal levels of weight or height for age.

Details of the catch-up in weight were available in 8 out of the 13 studies. In only Studies 1 and 8 was there no catch-up in weight on prolonged follow-up, but the controls were not siblings in Study 1 and in Study 8 there were significant social and environmental problems in the index group as compared with the controls. In Studies 2, 6, 7, 10, 12 and 13 there were no differences demonstrated between the index cases and the control groups and the follow-up weights varied from the third percentile to the 25th percentile. Siblings were used for comparison in Studies 10 and 13 and these findings could be criticized as not being representative of the full catch-up potential as the whole family could have been suffering from malnutrition. Nevertheless, Studies 2, 6, 7 and 12 showed no difference in catch-up growth when compared with nonsibling controls.

In summary, when social and environmental factors are less important, the majority of these studies show an ability for catch-up growth in weight although the weights are in the lower percentiles when compared with American standards.

Head circumference

A single normal head circumference (one within two standard deviations above or below the mean for age and sex) may prove misleading since it gives no clue as to the rate of head growth[32]. O'Connell *et al.*[34] showed that children with a head circumference below minus 2 standard deviations from the normal (3rd percentile) are with few exceptions mentally subnormal. They were unable to demonstrate a linear relationship between mental subnormality and decreasing head size (i.e. the smaller the head size, the lower the IQ). Other important variables relevant to the correlation between brain size and measurement of the head circumference were discussed previously.

Stein and Susser[86] showed that prenatal exposure to the Dutch Famine of 1944–45 reduced head circumference at birth by 2.7% during the famine, and rose by 2.4% afterward. The data on the effects of malnutrition on head circumference is best documented for the premature infant. It is generally accepted that premature infants do not achieve normal body proportions until the age of 2 years[87]. Davies and Davis[88] reported on 120 infants with low birth weights. Thirty-eight of these were small for dates (SFD) and had a mean birth weight of

1310 g and a mean gestational age of 239 days. The second category (82 infants) whose birth weights were appropriate for dates (AFD) had a mean birth weight of 1278 g and a mean gestational age of 208 days. The analysis was split into two eras: 1961–1964 and 1965–1968. The latter period was marked by more liberal feeding and greater attention to thermal regulation. Plots of the percentile distributions showed the head circumference to be low in the SFD and AFD groups 1961–1964. On the other hand, in the 1965–1968 period there was a normal distribution amongst the AFD group but a skewed distribution among the SFD group. This focuses attention on the fetal environment during the second and third trimesters of pregnancy and on the need for intensive attention to the nutrition of premature infants. This is a complicated problem and we should be more involved with the *quality* of the nutrition rather than attempting to achieve maximum growth. Indeed there is evidence that too high a protein intake in the premature results in hyperaminoacidaemia and unknown consequences to the development of the brain[89]. Obviously there were other factors resulting in the improvement in neonatal care during these two eras that could act as alternative variables and have been responsible for some of these differences. Fitzhardinge and Steven[90] followed 96 small-for-dates infants prospectively for 4 or more years. At birth the infants had a gestational age of 38 weeks or greater and a birth weight 30% or more below the average for their gestational age. The length and head circumference of the infants at birth showed a wider range than weight, suggesting that skull growth was relatively less affected by intrauterine growth retardation than body weight. At 6 years of age only 8% had a height greater than the 50th percentile, whereas 35% were on or below the 3rd percentile. Both at birth and at 4 years there was a highly significant positive correlation between length and head circumference, suggesting, though not proving, that catch-up skull growth had also occurred.

Bjerre[91] reported on a prospective investigation of the physical growth of children with a low birth weight (LBW) up to 5 years of age. The children had all been born and received their medical care in Malmo, Sweden, and socio–economic factors were not considered important in the population studied. The growth of the low birth weight children was slightly retarded in respect of stature, weight and osseous development but not regarding head circumference. The values found for stature and osseous development were low in the group small for gestational age and for twins. Those LBW children who were appropriate for gestational age developed at a normal rate. It was concluded that the physical development of the children varied most with the mother's stature and weight and probably with hereditary factors.

Prospective longitudinal studies on head circumference are unavailable in some of the classic studies on catch-up growth in malnutrition[76] or even in the follow-up of children malnourished from celiac disease[77]. Graham and Adrizien[78], in studies of malnourished infants in Peru, found that the head circumference in nearly all cases was between two standard deviations of the mean for height age. In those children where linear growth accelerated markedly after 'adaptation' the head kept pace with height, suggesting the existence of an equal potential for delayed catch-up. They did not notice, however, an improvement in IQ to parallel or match those observed in height and head size and stressed the importance of severe and prolonged deprivation in early life and its effect on IQ.

Data on the follow-up of head circumference was available in five out of thirteen studies. In Study 1 the average head circumference of the 20 patients in the malnourished group was significantly smaller by 2.46 cm than the controls after an 11-year follow-up. Moreover the head circumference of the controls compared favourably with that of American children. All patients were from a low socio–economic class in South Africa. In Study 6 the head circumference of 14 infants from a lower social group in Chile followed up over a 3–6 year period was also found to be below normal. Study 7 could find no difference on follow-up between undernourished subjects and controls 8–11 years after an episode of malnutrition in India. In Study 8 no significant differences for weight or head circumference between children admitted prior to 4 months of age and their controls were demonstrated, but height, weight and head circumference were all low on a 3-year follow-up in those infants admitted to hospital after the age of 4 months. Study 13 in a follow-up 2–21 years after an episode of malnutrition found the mean head circumference to be on the 12th percentile and comparable with the height and weight parameters.

In summary, there does appear to be substantial data that in a lower socio–economic environment and where the duration and severity of the malnutrition are extensive, permanent deficits in head circumference are usually found. Where malnutrition can be more isolated from other complicating variables recovery in head circumference may be possible.

INTELLECTUAL DEVELOPMENT

Assessment of intelligence

During infancy and early childhood a child passes through stages of development which usually succeed one another and are age-related. In contrast the retarded child may be delayed and/or frozen in one of these stages. The types of behaviour that characterize these stages can be measured and form the basis of the Gesell and other developmental assessments. These scales consist of items reflecting general alertness, perceptual motor status and imitative activity; hence they may more appropriately be considered tests of *developmental progress* rather than of intelligence as measured in the Stanford–Binet and the Weschler Intelligence Scale for older children (WISC).

Infant scales are quite invalid as measures of future potential and it is also unlikely that they properly assess a child's current performance vis-à-vis the other children[92]. Intelligence test scores are widely used in the evaluation of infant intervention or enrichment programmes. The data on infant intelligence tests cast doubt on whether the scores have any generalized applicability beyond the particular set of abilities or factors sampled at the time of testing. For example, an infant who showed dramatic gains in tests involving sensory motor functions would not necessarily manifest such gains in tests involving verbal skills. Infant intelligence cannot be considered as a general unitary trait but is rather a composite of differing skills and abilities[92]. This view of intelligence is necessary to counteract the tendency to utilize simple and single measures of infant intelligence when assessing the intellectual development of malnourished children.

Although scores in tests given to infants and children of *pre-school age* are poor predictors of scores reached on sensory, motor, speech or intelligence tests later in life, scores in intelligence tests given to children of *school age* are much better predictors of later test performance in that particular cultural setting. Intelligence tests are assembled pragmatically, however, and the items draw upon knowledge gained in the past. Opportunities to acquire a common set of experiences differ between social groups in any one society and more radically between societies. Applying formal intelligence tests to children in different cultures tells us about their relative performance on a particular test, but are not informative about the true abilities of the children in real life situations. Yarborough *et al.*[93] favour the use of specific tests to measure specific functions in a manner which is valid to the population being studied. The testing of specific behavioural competences is informative but even the tests of intersensory organization devised by Birch and Lefford[94] have given equivocal or contradictory findings in six studies[95]. Klein *et al.*[95] speculate that poor performance on this test is brought about by impulsiveness and not poorer intellectual capacity. Only prospective studies can confirm that increased impulsiveness is an effect and not a cause of malnutrition. Tizard[96] concluded that the available evidence does not enable us to decide which is the best of the various hypotheses that have been proposed to account for the failure of most disadvantaged children to do well on most cognitive tests. That such children do tend to perform badly is, however, well established.

Clarke and Clarke[97] discussed the relationship of mental retardation and behavioural change and noted that all epidemiological studies indicate the highest prevalence of a mildly subnormal population towards the end of the schooling period of life. Thereafter the number identified dropped dramatically, sometimes by 50%. Thus many of these subnormal conditions appear to be self-limiting, and it seems that in terms of adverse social factors, society may undo or allow to be undone, the damaging effect it produced earlier in life—factors which in childhood and under special circumstances appear to be associated with a detriment in IQ. They postulated three mechanisms to account for the changing status of some of these persons from adolescence onwards.

(a) *Camouflage*—The later years in school are more intellectually challenging than thereafter and hence intellectual limitations are more obvious. No behavioural change is necessarily involved.

(b) *Prolonged learning*—The mildly subnormal person is a slow learner but gradually acquires the skills necessary for adaptation to the community. With growing competence he becomes no longer what he was and thus behavioural change is involved.

(c) *Delayed maturation*—A number of studies indicate that at least in some culturally deprived people, improvement (including IQ increments) occurs in adolescence and early adult life. This appears to be as much a process of recovery from past damage as a responsiveness to a better situation. In some cases improvements of 20 or 30 points in IQ are noted.

Social follow-up of deprived subnormal subjects indicates that gradual improvement occurs. Groups that at school age were markedly homogeneous with respect to intelligence, scholastic handicap and social status become increasingly heterogeneous on later follow-up even without any special intervention[98]. Where intervention is extensive and prolonged, dramatic differences in outcome between children subjected to experiments and those acting as controls are revealed[99]. Jensen[100] reviewed the Head Start programme and stated that compensatory education has been tried and apparently has failed (in his view for intractable genetic reasons). Several programmes have, however, been effective. Heber and Garber[101] developed a programme for retarded slum dwelling mothers and their newborn babies for whom there was a high risk of developing subsequent mental retardation. These children were removed from their homes from the age of 3 months for 5 days a week and subjected to intensive programmes of perceptual, language and problem solving stimulation for 6 years. The results showed that when compared with controls their development was accelerated to an average IQ of 120–130 at the age of $3\frac{1}{2}$ years. By the age of 6 or 7 years, when the intervention programme had ceased, there was an average decline in IQ of the experimental group to 112 at age 6 and 110 at age 7[102]. This data demonstrates that intervention programmes require (1) a long duration, probably of the order of 12–15 years, to be effective; (2) they must include the child's family or shift to an adoptive family; (3) they must be highly structured; (4) they must be subsequently reinforced.

Discussion of the merits, reliability and indications for specific intelligence tests are discussed in detail in Chapter 4. Summarizing the preceding discussion it can be stated that among mildly subnormal subjects there are some who undergo spontaneous changes in selective development. Such changes can also be induced by calculated environmental manipulation. There is also no reason to doubt the existence of genetically determined limits although these may be less narrow than previously thought. Unless social factors are taken into account, initial assessment by itself gives poor long-term prediction. Possible aetiologies for intellectual impairment differ in emphasis from congenital through biological insult to social deprivation. Prospective studies are necessary to elucidate the cause-and-effect relationship between these variables.

Studies of infants and pre-school children

Five of the thirteen studies investigated the intellectual development of infants and pre-school children (Table 5.4). The age of the nutritional insult was usually under 1 year. Follow-up varied from 1–5 years where pre-school intelligence quotient was analysed although some of these studies have now extended their follow-up to 8–21 years. The tests used for intellectual assessment are shown in Table 5.4.

Table 5.4 Showing results of intelligence tests performed on infants and pre-school children recovered from malnutrition

Study	Age Malnutrition	Intelligence test	Result
1	10–16 mos.	Merrill Palmer	Index 70·9 Control 93·5 $p < 0.01$
		Gesell	Index 68 Control 92
3	< 6 mos.	Gesell	Significantly ↓ (*No controls*)
6	3–11 mos.	Gesell	Significantly ↓ (*No controls*)
		Binet (N 90–110)	Mean 62
8	1–12 mos.	Yale Rev. Dev. Exam	Control 99·4 Index 95·1 (< 4 mos.) Index 70·3 (> 4 mos.) $p < 0.01$
13	< 6 mos.	Merrill Palmer (N 70–79)	Index 40 Control 70 $p < 0.005$

The Merrill Palmer test showed significant differences between index cases and controls in Studies 1 and 13. In Study 1 both controls and index cases scored below the normal whereas in Study 13 controls and index cases scored within the average values for the test. Item analysis in Study 1 showed significant differences in the subtests of vocabulary, problems, pattern completion, blocks and form board. Item analysis in

Study 13 showed significant deficits in tests of fine motor function[103].

The Gesell test was used in Studies 1, 3 and 6 and showed significant deficits in all studies in the malnourished children. No controls were used in Studies 3 or 6. In Study 3 as the patients recovered from malnutrition, the difference between the chronological age and the developmental age in the fields of adaptive, motor, language and personal social behaviour was found to decrease, except in the group of children whose chronological age on admission was below 6 months. In these patients the initial deficit remained constant during the entire observation period which was sometimes up to 6 months. In Study 6 the most significant deficit was in language followed by adaptive ability, whereas the best performance of these children was in the field of personal–social relationships. In Study 6 the children tested by the Gesell method were divided into three groups according to height, on the assumption that children experiencing the more prolonged and sustained malnutrition would show the greatest retardation in growth. The separate Gesell test areas show different grades of subnormality especially in children below the 10th percentile in height. Furthermore, the group of well nourished children in poor socio–economic circumstances also included a high proportion of subnormal individuals. The authors concluded that socio–economic factors strongly affect mental development and cannot be separated satisfactorily from nutritional influences.

The Yale Revised Developmental Examination examines the developmental quotient and includes standardized items from the Gesell developmental scale, Stanford–Binet, Form L-M, Merrill Palmer mental test and the Hetzer–Wolff infant test. The Yale Revised Developmental Examination was used in Study 8 with a mean follow-up period of $3\frac{1}{2}$ years. The controls' score of 99 did not differ significantly from those infants malnourished before the age of 4 months who had a score of 95. Significant differences were found when the scores were compared with those infants malnourished and admitted to hospital *after* the age of 4 months who had a score of 70. All five areas of development were statistically lower ($p < 0.01$). The lowest score was in the field of language (score = 60), followed by gross motor (score = 70), adaptive (score = 73) and fine motor (score = 87). It is important to realize that 15 out of 19 of the children were of Spanish American descent, and this deficit in language must be interpreted with caution.

The Binet Scale was used in Study 6 and showed the mean intelligence quotient was 62 and never above 76 by 3–6 years of age (normal 90–110). Item analysis of the same group of children was discussed previously when the results of the Gesell testing procedure were analysed.

In summary, the results of a variety of tests of intellectual or developmental quotients of infants and pre-school children show consistent delay in the performance of the malnourished children when compared with controls. In deprived populations the scores of both index cases and controls fall below the norm and item analysis shows that language and adaptive behaviour are most affected. When the population comes from the middle social classes the data shows that their performance may be within the normal range but is significantly lower than their sibling controls. Under these circumstances item analysis demonstrates that the major difference lies in non-language tests of fine motor function.

These findings would be compatible with previous data showing that in deprived populations the predominant effect is on the acquisition of language. In animals the cerebellum is one of the most vulnerable areas of the brain to nutritional insult and is involved in the control of fine motor function. Data on the vulnerability of the cerebellum to nutritional insult in the human is incomplete, but would appear to be similar to the data in animals[60].

Studies of children over 5 years of age

Ten of the 13 studies investigated the intellectual development of children over 5 years of age (Table 5.5). The WISC was performed in six studies and shows conflicting data with a significant difference between the malnourished group and controls in Studies 1, 9 and 11 and no significant difference noted in Studies 5, 10 and 13. A feature of these studies was the low performance of the control groups with only Study 13 having results in the normally accepted range. The Goodenough draw-a-man test was performed in three studies (Studies 5, 10 and 12) and showed a significant difference in one out of the three studies. Modifications of the Stanford–Binet test were performed on two occasions (Studies 1 and 2) and showed significant differences between the malnourished group and controls. The tests of intersensory integrative ability devised by Birch and Lefford[94] showed significant differences between the two groups in Studies 4 and 7.

Table 5.5 Showing results of intelligence tests performed on patients over 5 years of age who have recovered from malnutrition

Studies	Age malnutrition (Months)	Age testing (Years)	Intelligence test *Modified	Scores	Significance	Comments/Correlations
1	10–16	11	Stanford Binet*	I 71 C 95	$p < 0.01$	Controls very low ($N = 90$–110)
			WISC*	I 61 C 77	$p < 0.01$	
2	4–24	7–14	Binet Simon	I 88 C 105	$p < 0.01$	1. No correlation between age malnutrition and subsequent IQ 2. Correlation between deficit in expected weight for age on admission and IQ on follow-up
4	24–48	6–11	Birch and Lefford	Intersensory Integrative Ability ↓	Significantly	Upper social class sample demonstrated no differences in intersensory ability and height measurements.
5		5–12	WISC	I 75 C 77	NS	Correlation of IQ and severity of malnutrition
			Goodenough	I 77 C 82	$p < 0.01$	

			Devised	Index Mean 31–52% of Controls (Significant)		
7	18–36	8–11	Birch and Lefford			All differences less with age. Verbal and Performance data similar.
9	6–30	5–13	WISC	I 68 / C 81	p < 0·01	
10	10–36	10	WISC	I 77 / C 78	NS	No correlation between IQ scores and height and weight at time of testing.
			Goodenough	I 76 / C 80	NS	
11	3–24	5–10	WISC	I 58 / C (Siblings) 62 / C (Comparison) 66	$p < 0·025$ / $p < 0·001$	1. Performance IQ shows *no* significant difference between Index and Controls 2. No association IQ and age of hospitalization for malnutrition
12	1–22	3–14	Goodenough	I 106 / C 100	NS	Correlation between lowest IQ scores and longest duration of hospitalization.
13	1–6	2–21	WISC	I 101 / C 104	NS	

There was no correlation between the age of malnutrition or hospitalization and the subsequent IQ in Studies 2 and 11 and yet Study 12 showed that the children with the lowest scores had been hospitalized for the longest period in the first 2 years. Studies 2 and 5 showed a correlation between the nutritional deficits on the original admission and the IQ on subsequent examination. Study 4 could show correlations between IQ performance and height measurements in the rural population but not with an upper social class population. Study 10 on the other hand could find no correlation between IQ scores and height and weight at the time of testing.

Where significant differences on intellectual assessment were demonstrated these included full-scale quotient, verbal quotient and performance quotient, and in the subtests of vocabulary, problems, pattern completion, blocks and form board (Study 1). Similar findings were demonstrated in Studies 9 and 11 except that in Study 11 the performance IQ showed no difference between index cases and siblings. One of the constant findings was the tendency for differences in the testing procedures to diminish with increasing age especially in those studies with a follow-up of 10–15 years.

In summary, the data on the intellectual development of school age children who suffered a period of malnutrition in infancy is once again conflicting. Most of the studies demonstrate a low performance even in the sibling and control groups. The results may include a generalized reduction in performance with a wide variety of testing procedures. Where the social functioning and nutritional status of the population being studied is higher, there is less evidence for impairment in intellectual functioning. Some studies were unable to demonstrate any significant deficits in IQ in the malnourished group. In all groups the differences decrease with time and emphasize the need for prolonged prospective studies to further delineate the role of malnutrition under these circumstances.

DISCUSSION

This chapter has reviewed the findings from clinical studies on the intellectual status of children and young adults who were severely malnourished in infancy. Only those studies, largely in the English language, that have made significant contributions to this subject were selected. Knowledge of the history of protein–calorie malnutrition is important for a proper perspective on the problem. In the 1950s the interrelationship of infection and malnutrition was of paramount importance in terms of survival from the malnutrition. Most of the early investigators ascribed the poor functioning on the tests of intellectual ability to the low socio–economic environment which was invariably present. In the 1960s a reappraisal of the human problem became relevant as a result of the findings on the effects of malnutrition on the animal brain and several well designed studies were undertaken in developing countries. The hypothesis was developed that children malnourished as infants suffer permanent brain damage and themselves become the parents of another deprived subnormal population. The social and political implications of this hypothesis were obvious and resulted in the funding of several studies to investigate the problem. Unfortunately many of these later studies have been influenced by social and political pressures and statements have been made that could not be substantiated from the scientific data. Recently several malnourished populations in developed countries have been studied and these findings must be taken into account before coming to conclusions. One consistent and recurring criticism is the lack of prospective studies in this field. If more of the early investigators had had the benefit of a historical perspective, then we would now be in possession of more meaningful data to answer some of these difficult questions.

Discussion of the evaluation of the nutritional status is essential before comparing studies on malnourished populations. The lack of a satisfactory biochemical test for malnutrition suitable for use in all parts of the world is noted, and a suggestion is made for the development of a multiple computerized scoring system for the assessment of the malnutrition syndromes. The merits and disadvantages of the various anthropometric measurements are discussed. Measurements of weight, height and head circumference and their relationship to age are the most important parameters. The age of the child may be unknown, however, and this is one example of the problems inherent in investigating a deprived population in a developing country. Most of the studies reviewed have used the Boston or some similar standard from developed countries that may not be relevant to the local population. Serial head circumference measurements (in contrast to weight and height measurements) of malnourished children have been deficient in many studies until recent years, in part reflecting a lack of priority in attention to the psychological parameters of their illness. Furthermore, head circumference is an indirect measure of brain volume and has been shown to be an unreliable guide to brain composition in experimental animal undernutrition. Thus methods which would permit an *in vivo* appreciation of the status of the human brain would have special significance. Transillumination and echo-encephalography are examples of these other techniques. Echo-encephalography has demonstrated significant increases in the size of the cerebral ventricles in children with kwashiorkor[38]. The increased transillumination found in malnourished infants in Chile[39] denotes cerebral atrophy with associated mental subnormality but the question is raised as to how this cerebral atrophy occurred. Three possibilities arise: (1) The brain failed to grow secondary to malnutrition. (2) The findings are the result of vascular thrombosis secondary to dehydration and gastroenteritis. (3) The child was the victim of child abuse and a subdural haematoma. The answer as to which of these possibilities is correct is unknown, but the hypothesis that the cerebral atrophy was caused by malnutrition alone (as stated by several investigators) is *not* yet substantiated and serious consideration must be given to the other two possibilities.

We have analysed the data on the effects of malnutrition on intellectual development by selecting 13 studies representative of several different parts of the world. There were 13 studies (Studies 1–13) considered to have been well controlled investigations and to have made significant contributions to an understanding of the subject. A list of the variables encountered in a study of intelligence after malnutrition was selected. A general discussion of each variable was followed by the specific data from the 13 studies when this was available. These findings were then summarized. By this method we have attempted to compare data that is frequently incomplete for all the thirteen studies. Moreover conclusions based on inadequate evidence can easily be identified (Table 5.3).

The importance of the socio-economic environment has been constantly stressed and relates also to parental IQ, sibling abilities, prenatal and post-natal factors. Furthermore socio-economic deprivation aggravates the effects of prolonged hospitalizations or the presence of other chronic diseases. The social conditions in which learning is least conducive to optimal mental development are generally similar to those in which the poorest level of nutrition is likely to exist. Moreover the same environments characterized by poor social and nutritional factors co-exist with the problems of inadequate antenatal care, poor hygiene, multiple infections such as the cytomegalovirus and a high infant mortality rate. The central nervous system may be vulnerable to all these associated factors and these must be ruled out before the cause and role of poor nutrition in the production of impaired mental development can be clearly established. Stein *et al.*[54] commented on the strong association of social class with mental performance in their studies on the effects of the Dutch famine. Whereas the effects of birth order are consistent across all social classes[53], the effect of family size was not present in all social classes. As family size increased the level of ability declined and this effect was strongest in the manual and less marked in the non-manual group. Data on family size and birth order is unknown in almost all studies of malnourished infants but we do know that the vast majority come from the lower social classes. Ten of the 13 studies discussed were from the lower social classes. Furthermore two of the three studies that came from an average social class background were unable to demonstrate any impairment in IQ at intervals of over 5 years from the date of the nutritional insult.

Parental IQ is closely associated with social class and socio-economic status. It is also known that environmental pressures play an important role in the determination of a child's IQ score. The data on parental IQ was only recorded in three out of 13 studies with a wide variation in results; thus this information was inadequate to form any conclusions. *The absence of data on parental IQ in a study on this subject is a serious criticism and mitigates the importance of some of the conclusions that may be drawn from this data.*

The characteristics of the control group in any study on malnourished children deserves close attention. The merits and disadvantages of using siblings as controls are discussed and the inclusion of a third comparison group is suggested. An alternative method that may be used in developed countries would be to study children with diseases such as cystic fibrosis or congenital malformations of the gastrointestinal tract that resulted in gross malnutrition and to compare these subjects with their healthy unaffected siblings. The data showed that four of the 13 studies used siblings as controls and the results were conflicting.

The findings were suggestive that the siblings in the majority of these studies were themselves subclinically malnourished.

The importance of prenatal, obstetric and neonatal factors in influencing subsequent intellectual development has been fully reviewed in Chapter 2. The fact that *the prenatal history was absent in all, the birthweight was only known in 5 of the 13 studies, the average birthweight was only 2.48 kg in Study 8, and that the gestational age and neonatal progress were only documented in two studies*, are all examples of the *inadequacy of this important data from the majority of studies reviewed*. Nevertheless many of these same investigators have concluded that malnutrition *per se* caused the demonstrated mental impairment.

The importance of the critical period of vulnerability of the brain has been well reviewed[62] and we now realize that $\frac{5}{6}$ of the human brain growth spurt is postnatal and thus resembles the rat. Some of the earlier studies were performed at a time that investigators believed that the human brain growth spurt was perinatal and thus resembled the pig. Many of these investigators believed that it was only during the first 6 months of life that the brain was vulnerable to nutritional damage and that after this period there was little risk from nutritional insult. The new findings on the quantitative growth and development of the human brain[36] have not only contradicted this earlier view but have also suggested that the cerebellum may be one of the areas of the brain most prone to nutritional insult. Although animal experiments have tended to involve degrees of malnutrition more severe than is usually found in the human, the findings in malnourished animals demonstrated a reduced brain size especially of the cerebellum, fewer cells by DNA analysis, less cerebral lipid especially those characterized by myelin and altered brain enzyme activity. The number of studies on the malnourished human brain are still too limited in number, as well as being characterized by numerous complicating variables, to enable us to come to any definite conclusions. The data on the earlier critical period of neuroblast multiplication (10–18 weeks) is and probably always will remain elusive. Our data on the low brain weights of malnourished infants dying of cystic fibrosis with meconium ileus are similar to other reported studies on human and animal brains. In the future most of our knowledge on the effect of malnutrition in the brain will have to be extrapolated from animal data, whereas the effects of malnutrition on intelligence will require appropriate testing of mental abilities in the human. Eleven of the 13 studies investigated children who were initially malnourished under 2 years of age in the so-called critical period. The results show conflicting results with wide variability. Furthermore it is impossible to form any conclusions as to whether malnutrition in the first 6 months or the second year causes a different effect. Nevertheless *there is suggestive evidence that the longer or the more severe the malnutrition, the more serious the effect on intellectual development.*

This review has stressed the important influence of a period of hospitalization on the psychological development of the child. Eleven of the 13 studies involved a period of hospitalization for the malnourished child with a range of 16 to 360 days. *This variability of duration of hospitalization is highly significant* even in studies that attributed all the poor performance to the effects of malnutrition (e.g. Study 3) and *may be one of the more important factors accounting for the wide variability in results.* The effects of isolation and neglect that may result from such a prolonged period in hospital or institution is discussed further in Chapter 6. In societies where the parents can either live with their child or assist in his daily care during hospitalization, this may not be such an important factor, but there is no indication from the data that is given that this policy was practised in most of the studies.

Chronic diseases such as congenital heart lesions have sometimes been shown to produce significant deficits in intellectual functioning[68, 69], and lead to psychological maladjustments[67]. Moreover even when intellectual functioning may be normal, deficits in academic functioning may be noted[71]. Despite these interesting effects only two of the 13 studies (Studies 12 and 13) involved children with chronic diseases (cystic fibrosis and gastrointestinal tract anomalies) and in neither of these two studies could any overall diminution in intellectual performance be demonstrated on prolonged follow-up.

Assessment of recovery from malnutrition is largely of academic interest in terms of height and weight, whereas follow-up of recovery of head circumference and intellectual development is of enormous practical import. A failure of recovery at follow-up in either of the 3 anthropometric parameters (height, weight and head circumference) may indicate continuing chronic subnutrition and a failure of catch-up

potential. The literature and data from Studies 1 to 13 shows conflicting results in catch-up height (5 out of 8 studies showed catch-up,
where 3 out of 8 failed to demonstrate this achievement). The figures
for recovery in weight were more encouraging with 6 out of 8 showing
full recovery although the values still tended to lie in the lower percentile for the American standards. Ashworth[85] has detailed the growth
rate with recovery from protein–calorie malnutrition in Jamaica when
children remain in hospital for at least 3 months. She showed that
once a child with protein–caloric malnutrition has reached the expected
weight for height, he will tend voluntarily to regulate downwards his
food intake. Under normal circumstances children with kwashiorkor
and marasmus are discharged much earlier and long before normal
weight for height is achieved. This may account for the fact that many
of these children never reach normal levels of weight or height for
age. Interestingly follow-up studies of height and weight are some of
the few recordings that have been made in a prospective form and
thus are more meaningful for interpretation.

Data on the recovery of head circumference in malnutrition is ac-
cumulating although this is still rather inadequate when compared with
that documented for height and weight. Stein *et al.*[86] showed that
prenatal exposure to the Dutch famine of 1944–45 reduced the head
circumference at birth by 2.7% during the famine and rose by 2.4%
afterwards. The findings of Davies and Davis[88] on the follow-up of
premature infants documented the importance of gestational age and
neonatal nutritional practices. The small for gestational age infants had
a significantly higher incidence of intellectual impairment. We now
know that intrauterine growth retardation results in significant decreases
in ultimate head circumference and an increased incidence of neurological deficits when compared with the findings in infants of normal
birth weight. Data on the follow-up of the head circumference was
available in 5 of the 13 studies and 3 of them showed a failure of catch-up
in head circumference. These findings are extremely important in view
of the known association between a decreased head size and mental
subnormality. *Impaired intellectual functioning was demonstrated in all
those studies where the follow-up head circumference was significantly
reduced. However data on gestational age is absent and the possibility that
intrauterine growth retardation was responsible is not excluded.*

Before discussing the results of intelligence tests on specific malnourished populations, we have reviewed some general principles relating to the value, applicability and significance to be attached to a particular group of tests. This subject is discussed in greater detail in Chapter 4. We must again emphasize that scores in tests given to infants and children of pre-school age are poor predictors of scores reached on sensory, motor, speech or intelligence tests later in life, whereas scores in IQ tests given to children of school age are much better predictors of later test performance in that particular cultural setting. Applying formal intelligence tests to children in different cultures tells us about their relative performance in a particular test, but are not informative about the true abilities of the children in real life situations. The use of specific tests to measure a specific function in a manner valid to the population being studied has been devised, such as Birch and Lefford's Test of Intersensory Organization[94], and yet even this test has given equivocal or contradictory findings in six studies. Klein *et al.*[95] suggest that the poor performance on this test was related to impulsiveness but whether this is an effect and not a cause of malnutrition can only be answered by prospective studies. Tizard[96] has concluded that the available evidence does not enable us to decide which hypothesis accounts best for the fact that most disadvantaged children fail to perform well on most tests of cognitive function. The controversy on the effects of early intervention programmes and their effect on intelligence continues. We now know that intervention programmes require a long duration probably of the order of 12–15 years to be effective, they must include the child's family or shift to an adoptive family, they must be highly structured and they must be subsequently reinforced. Where one is dealing with a *markedly deprived population, one must realize that slow but gradual improvement in both IQ increments and social adaptation occurs in adolescence and early adult life*[97]. *Thus allowance must be made for these possibilities especially where one is dealing with a culturally deprived lower social class population as is so common in studies of malnourished children.*

Tests of the intellectual or developmental quotient of infants and pre-school children were performed in 5 of the 13 studies and *showed consistent delay in the performance of the malnourished children when compared with controls* (Table 5.4). The Merrill Palmer test showed significant difference in two studies. Whereas in Study 1 both controls and index cases scored below normal, in Study 13 they were within the

normal range. Item analysis showed significant differences in the subtests of vocabulary, problem completion, blocks and form board in
Study 1 and similar tests of fine motor function in Study 13. The
Gesell test was used in 3 studies (Studies 1, 3 and 6) and showed the
most severe deficit was in language followed by adaptive ability,
whereas the best performance was in the field of personal–social relationships. The Yale Revised Developmental Examination and the
Binet scales showed similar findings. Several authors concluded that
socio-economic factors strongly affect mental development and cannot
be separated satisfactorily from nutritional influences. *In deprived
populations, the scores of both index cases and controls fall below the norm
and item analysis shows that language and adaptive behaviour are more
affected. When the study population comes from the middle social classes,
their performance may be within the normal range, but is still significantly lower than their controls and item analysis shows that this difference lies in non-language tests of fine motor function. The latter findings
would be compatible with experimental data in rats indicating that the
cerebellum is the area of the brain most prone to nutritional insults* and
that *this is manifested by decreased performance in tests of fine motor
function.*

Ten of the 13 studies investigated the intellectual development of
children over 5 years of age (Table 5.5). The WISC was performed in
6 studies and showed conflicting results with three studies showing
significant differences and three showing no difference between index
and controls. The Goodenough draw-a-man test showed a significant
difference in 1 out of 3 studies. Both the Stanford–Binet (two studies)
and the Birch and Lefford test of intersensory integrative ability
showed significant differences between the malnourished group and the
normal. When significant differences on intellectual assessment were
demonstrated these included full scale quotient, verbal quotient and
performance quotient and in the subtests of vocabulary, problems,
pattern completion, blocks and form board (Study 1). Similar findings
were present in Studies 9 and 11 except that performance IQ showed
no difference between index cases and siblings in Study 11. *There was a
tendency for all differences on testing procedures to diminish with increasing
age especially in those studies extending up to 15 years.* These findings
are especially relevant to our earlier discussion of the effects of early
intervention programmes and the recommendation that these should

be continued for 12–15 years to be effective. *These findings in school age children are different from the findings in infants and pre-school children where all studies showed a significantly diminished performance in the malnourished group; in contrast in school age children at least 50% of the studies do not demonstrate significant intellectual deficits compared with their non-malnourished controls. Caution is necessary before extrapolating too much from this data as prospective studies have not been consistently performed and thus the question of whether recovery or compensation for deficits in intellectual performance occurred remains unanswered.* The fact that 50% of the studies could show no significant impairment on intellectual functioning and that these findings occurred more often when the study population came from the middle and upper social classes without evidence of socio–economic deprivation, is certainly reassuring. *The evidence suggests that recovery may be related to a combination of adequate nutritional replacement in association with much emotional and psychological support and that this is not only a continuous process but these different parameters also reinforce one another. Thus efforts to alleviate this situation in less fortunate areas of the world require not only nutritional replacement, but more emphasis on improvement in the emotional well being of the family.* Only in this way can some of the devastating effects of malnutrition on future psychological development be averted.

ACKNOWLEDGEMENTS

Special thanks are due to Mrs Joan Groh for secretarial assistance. The majority of the work was performed while the author was at The Pennsylvania State University College of Medicine, Hershey, Pennsylvania.

REFERENCES

1. Trowell, H. C., Davies, J. N. P. and Dean, R. F. A. (1954). *Kwashiorkor.* (London: Edward Arnold)
2. Williams, C. D. (1933). A nutritional disease of childhood associated with a maize diet. *Arch. Did. Childh.,* **8**, 423
3. Williams, C. D. (1935). Kwashiorkor: A nutritional disease of children associated with a maize diet. *Lancet,* **ii**, 1151
4. Brock, J. F. and Autret, M. (1952). *Kwashiorkor in Africa.* (Geneva: WHO Monograph Series, N. 8)

5. Waterlow, J. C. (1948). Fatty liver disease in infants in the British West Indies. *Med. Research Council Spec. Rept. No. 263* (U.K.)

6. Oomen, H. A. P. C. (1953). A survey on malignant malnutrition in Djakarta toddlers. *Institute of Nutrition* (Djakarta, Indonesia)

7. Gopalan, C. and Ramalingaswami, V. (1955). Kwashiorkor in India. *Indian J. Med. Res.*, **43**, 751

8. Gomez, F., Ramos-Galvan, R. and Cravioto, J. (1955). Malnutrition in infancy and childhood, with special reference to kwashiorkor. *Advan. Pediat.*, **7**, 131

9. Waterlow, J. C. and Scrimshaw, N. S. (1957). The concept of kwashiorkor from a public health point of view. *Bull. WHO*, **16**, 458

10. Scrimshaw, N. S., Taylor, C. E. and Gordon, J. E. (1959) Interactions of nutrition and infection. *Am. J. Med. Sci.*, **237**, 367

11. Waterlow, J. C., Cravioto, J. and Stephen, J. M. L. (1960). Protein malnutrition in man. *Adv. Protein Chem.*, **15**, 131

12. Geber, M. and Dean, R. F. A. (1956). Psychological changes accompanying kwashiorkor. *Courrier*, **6**, 3

13. Still, G. F. (1918). The Lumleian Lectures on coeliac disease. *Lancet*, **ii**, 163, 193, 227

14. McCance, R. A. and Widdowson, E. M. (1962). Nutrition and growth. *Proc. R. Soc. B.*, **156**, 326

15. Cowley, J. J. and Griesel, R. D. (1962). Pre and Post natal effects of low protein diet on the behaviour of the white rat. *Psychol. Africana*, **9**, 216

16. Barnes, R. H., Cunnold, S. R., Zimmerman, R. R., Simmons, H., MacLeod, R. B. and Krook, L. (1966). Influence of nutritional deprivations in early life on learning behaviour of rats as measured by performance in a water maze. *J. Nutr.*, **89**, 399

17. Widdowson, E. M. and McCance, R. A. (1960). Some effects of accelarating growth. I. General somatic development. *Proc. R. Soc. B.*, **152**, 88

18. Winick, M. (1970). Cellular growth in intrauterine malnutrition. *Pediatr. Clin. N. Am.*, **17**, 69

19. Scrimshaw, N. S. and Gordon, J. E. (1968). *Malnutrition, Learning and Behaviour* (Cambridge, Massachusetts: MIT Press)

20. Graham, G. G. (1968). In *Malnutrition, Learning and Behaviour*, (N. S. Scrimshaw and J. E. Gordon, editors) p. 84 (Cambridge, Massachusetts: MIT Press)

21. Latham, M. C. (1968). In *Malnutrition, Learning and Behaviour*, (N. S. Scrimshaw and J. E. Gordon, editors) p. 299 (Cambridge, Massachusetts: MIT Press)

22. Latham, M. C. (1974). Protein–calorie malnutrition in children and its relation to psychological development and behaviour. *Physiol. Rev.*, **54**, 541

23. Rubin, R. A., Rosenblatt, C. and Balow, B. (1973). Psychological and educational sequelae of prematurity. *Pediatrics*, **52**, 352

24. Naeye, R. L., Diener, M. M., Harcke, H. T., Jr. and Blanc, W. A. (1971). Relation of poverty and race to birth weight and organ and cell structure in the newborn. *Pediatr. Res.*, **5**, 17

25. Committee Report (1970). Assessment of protein nutritional status. *Amer. J. Clin. Nutr.*, **23**, 807

26. Owen, G. M., Kram, K. M., Garry, P. J., Lowe, J. E. and Lubin, A. H. (1974). A study of nutritional status of pre-school children in the United States 1968-1970. *Pediatrics*, **53** (Suppl.), 597

27. Jelliffe, D. B. (1966). *The Assessment of the Nutritional Status of the Community* (Geneva: WHO Monograph Series, No. 53)

28. Gomez, F., Ramos-Galvan, R., Frenk, S., Cravioto, J., Munoz, J. C., Chavez, R. and Vazquez, J. (1956). Mortality in second and third degree malnutrition. *J. Trop. Pediatr.*, **2**, 77

29. Editorial. (1970). Classification of infantile malnutrition. *Lancet*, **ii**, 302

30. Joint FAO/WHO Expert Committee on Nutrition. (1971). *Food Fortification Protein–Calorie Malnutrition*. (Geneva: WHO Technical Report Series No. 477)

31. Seone, N. and Latham, M. C. (1971). Nutritional anthropometry in the identification of malnutrition in childhood. *J. Trop. Pediatr. Env. Child Hlth*, **17**, 198

32. Nellhaus, G. (1968). Head circumference from birth to eighteen years. *Pediatrics*, **41**, 106

33. Terada, H. and Hoshi, H. (1965). Longitudinal study on the physical growth in Japanese. Growth in chest and head circumference during the first three years of life. *Acta Anat. Nippon*, **40**, 368

34. O'Connell, E. J., Feldt, R. H. and Stickler, G. B. (1965). Head circumference, mental retardation and growth failure. *Pediatrics*, **36**, 62

35. Sunderman, F. W. and Boerner, F. (1949). *Normal Values in Clinical Medicine*. (Philadelphia: W. B. Saunders)

36. Dobbing, J. and Sands, J. (1973). Quantitative growth and development of human brain. *Arch. Dis. Child.*, **48**, 757

37. Stern, H., Elek, S. D., Booth, J. C., and Fleck, D. G. (1969). Microbial causes of mental retardation. *Lancet*, **ii**, 443

38. Vahlquist, B., Engsner, G. and Sjogren, I. (1971). Malnutrition and size of the cerebral ventricles. *Acta Paediatr. Scand.*, **60**, 533

39. Mönckeburg, F. B. (1969). Malnutrition and mental behaviour. *Nutr. Rev.*, **27**, 191

40. Caffey, J. (1974). The whiplash shaken infant syndrome: Manual shaking by the extremities with whiplash-induced intracranial and intraocular bleedings, linked with residual permanent brain damage and mental retardation. *Pediatrics*, **54**, 396

41. Coppoletta, J. M. and Wolbach, S. B. (1933). Body length and organ weights of infants and children. *Am. J. Pathol.*, **9**, 55

42. Schulz, D. M., Giordano, D. A. and Schulz, D. H. (1962). Weights of organs of fetuses and infants. *Arch. Pathol.*, **74**, 244

43. Brown, R. E. (1965). Decreased brain weight in malnutrition and its implications. *East Afr. Med. J.*, **42**, 584

44. Brown, R. E. (1966). Organ weight in malnutrition with special reference to brain weight. *Devel. Med. Child Neurol.*, **8**, 512

45. Naeye, R. L. (1965). Organ and cellular development in congenital heart disease and in alimentary malnutrition. *J. Pediatr.*, **67**, 447

46. Naeye, R. L. (1967). Anatomic features of growth failure in congenital heart disease. *Pediatrics*, **39**, 433

47. Winick, M. and Rosso, P. (1969). The effect of severe early malnutrition on cellular growth of human brain. *Pediatr. Res.*, **3**, 181

48. Boyer, R. H. (1955). Low birth weight in fibrocystic disease of the pancreas. *Pediatrics*, **16**, 778

49. Lloyd-Still, J. D., Wolff, P. H., Hurwitz, I. and Shwachman, H. (1975). Studies on intellectual development after severe malnutrition in infancy in cystic fibrosis and other intestinal lesions. In *Proc. Ninth International Congress of Nutrition*. Vol. 2, p. 357 (Basel: S. Karger)

50. Eells, K. W. and Davis, A. (1951). *Intelligence and Cultural Differences: A Survey of Cultural Learning and Problem Solving*. (Chicago: University Chicago Press)

51. Richardson, S. A. (1968). The influence of social–environmental and nutritional factors on mental ability. In *Malnutrition, Learning and Behaviour*, (N. S. Scrimshaw and J. E. Gordon, editors) p. 346 (Cambridge, Massachusetts: MIT Press)

52. Widdowson, E. M. and McCance, R. A. (1975). A review: new thoughts on growth. *Pediatr. Res.*, **9**, 154

53. Belmont, L. and Marolla, F. A. (1973). Birth order, family size and intelligence. *Science*, **182**, 1096

54. Stein, Z., Susser, M., Saenger, G. and Marolla, F. (1972). Nutrition and mental performance. *Science*, **178**, 708

55. Kagan, J. and Moss, H. A. (1959). Parental correlates of child's I.Q. and height: A cross-validation of the Berkeley Growth Study results. *Child Devel.*, **30**, 325

56. Bayley, N. (1954). Some increasing parent-child similarities during the growth of children. *J. Educ. Psychol.*, **45**, 1

57. Latham, M. C. (1967). Growth of children after malnutrition. *Lancet*, **i**, 278

58. Davison, A. N. and Dobbing, J. (1966). Myelination as a vulnerable period in brain development. *Br. Med. Bull.*, **22**, 40

59. Dobbing, J. (1970). Undernutrition and the developing brain. *Am. J. Dis. Childh.*, **120**, 411

60. Dobbing, J. and Smart, J. L. (1974). Vulnerability of developing brain and behaviour. *Br. Med. Bull.*, **30**, 164

61. Dobbing, J. and Sands, J. (1970). Timing of neuroblast multiplication in developing human brain. *Nature (London)*, **226**, 639

62. Dobbing, J. (1974). The later growth of the brain and its vulnerability. *Pediatrics*, **53**, 2

63. Dobbing, J. and Sands, J. (1971). Vulnerability of developing brain. IX. The effect of nutritional growth retardation on the timing of the brain growth spurt. *Biol. Neonat.*, **19**, 363

64. Bowlby, J. (1960). Separation anxiety. *Int. J. Psychoanalysis.*, **41**, 89

65. Schaffer, H. R. and Callender, W. M. (1959). Psychologic effects of hospitalisation in infancy. *Pediatrics*, **24**, 528

66. Cravioto, J. and Robles, B. (1965). Evolution of adaptive and motor behaviour during rehabilitation from kwashiorkor. *Am. J. Orthopsychiat.* **35**, 449

67. Pless, I. B. and Roghmann, K. J. (1971). Chronic illness and its consequences: Observations based on three epidemiologic surveys. *J. Pediatr.*, **79**, 351

68. Rasof, B., Linde, L. M. and Dunn, O. J. (1967). Intellectual development in children with congenital heart disease. *Child Devel.*, **38**, 1043

69. Silbert, A., Wolff, P. H., Mayer, B., Rosenthal, A. and Nadas, A. S. (1969). Cyanotic heart disease and psychological development. *Pediatrics*, **43**, 192

70. Gayton, W. F. and Friedman, S. B. (1973). Psychosocial aspects of cystic fibrosis. *Am. J. Dis. Child.*, **126**, 856

71. Lawler, R. H., Nakielny, W. and Wright, N. A. (1966). Psychological implications of cystic fibrosis. *Can. Med. Ass. J.*, **94**, 1043

72. Spock, A. and Stedman, D. J. (1966). Psychologic characteristics of children with cystic fibrosis. *N.C. Med. J.*, **27**, 426

73. Kulczycki, L. L., Robinson, M. E. and Berg, C. M. (1969). Somatic and psychosocial factors relative to management of patients with cystic fibrosis. *Clin. Proc. Children's Hosp. D.C.*, **25**, 320

74. McCance, R. A. (1962) Food, growth and time. *Lancet*, **ii**, 621

75. Acheson, R. M., Fowler, G. B. and Janes, M. D. (1962). Effect of improved care on predicted adult height of undernourished children. *Nature (London)*, **194**, 735

76. Garrow, J. S. and Pike, M. C. (1967). The long term prognosis of severe infantile malnutrition. *Lancet*, **i**, 1

77. Barr, D. G. D., Shmerling, D. H. and Prader, A. (1972). Catch-up growth in malnutrition, studied in celiac disease after institution of gluten-free diet. *Pediatr. Res.*, **6**, 521

78. Graham, G. G. and Adrianzen, T. B. (1971). Late catch-up growth after severe infantile malnutrition. *Hopkins Med. J.*, **131**, 204

79. Hansen, J. D. L., Brinkman, G. L. and Bowie, M. D. (1965). Body composition in protein-calorie malnutrition. *S. Afr. Med. J.*, **39**, 491

80. James, W. P. T. (1968). Intestinal absorption in protein–calorie malnutrition. *Lancet*, **i**, 333

81. Hadden, D. R. (1967). Glucose, free fatty acid and insulin interrelations in kwashiorkor and marasmus. *Lancet*, **ii**, 589

82. Parra, A., Garza, C., Garza, Y., Saravia, J. L., Hazlewood, C. F. and Nichols, B. L. (1973). Changes in growth hormone, insulin, and thyroxine

values, and in energy metabolism of marasmic infants. *J. Pediatr.*, **82**, 133

83. Viteri, F. E., Flores, J. M., Alvarado, J. and Behar, M. (1973). Intestinal malabsorption in malnourished children before and during recovery. *Am. J. Digest. Dis.*, **18**, 201

84. Ashworth, A., Bell, R., James, W. P. T. and Waterlow, J. C. (1968). Calorie requirements of children recovering from protein–calorie malnutrition. *Lancet*, **ii**, 600

85. Ashworth, A. (1969). Growth rates in children recovering from protein–calorie malnutrition. *Br. J. Nutr.*, **23**, 835

86. Stein, Z. and Susser, M., (1975). The Dutch Famine, 1944-45, and the reproductive process. I. Effects on six indices at birth. *Pediatr. Res.*, **9**, 70

87. Woolley, P. V. and Valdecanas, L. Q. (1960). Growth of premature infants: Circumferential growth of the skull, increase in body length and the relation between these measurements during the first year. *J. Dis. Childh.*, **99**, 642

88. Davies, P. A. and Davis, J. P. (1970). Very low birth-weight and subsequent head growth. *Lancet*, **ii**, 1216

89. Raiha, N. C. R. (1974). Biochemical basis for nutritional management of preterm infants. *Pediatrics*, **53**, 147

90. Fitzhardinge, P. M. and Steven, E. M. (1972). The small for date infant. I. Later growth patterns. *Pediatrics*, **49**, 671

91. Bjerre, J. (1975). Physical growth of 5-year-old children with a low birth weight. *Acta Paediatr. Scand.*, **64**, 33

92. Lewis, M. (1973). Infant intelligence tests: Their use and misuse. *Human Develop.*, **16**, 108

93. Yarbrough, C., Lasky, R. E., Habicht, J. P. and Klein, R. E. (1974). In *Early Malnutrition and Mental Development*. (J. Cravioto, L. Hambraeus and B. Vahlquist, editors) Symposium of the Swedish Nutrition Foundation No. XII. (Stockholm: Almqvist and Wiksell)

94. Birch, H. G. and Lefford, A. (1967). Visual differentiation, intersensory integration and voluntary motor control. *Monogr. Soc. Res. Child. Dev.*, **32**, No. 2

95. Klein, R. E., Habicht, J. P. and Yarbrough, C. (1971). Effects of protein–calorie malnutrition on mental development. *Adv. Pediatr.*, **18**, 75

96. Tizard, J. (1974). Early malnutrition, growth and mental development in man. *Br. Med. Bull.*, **30**, 169

97. Clarke, A. D. B. and Clarke, A. M. (1974). Mental retardation and behavioural change. *Br. Med. Bull.*, **30**, 179

98. Kennedy, R. J. A Connecticut community revisited: A study of the social adjustment of a group of mentally deficient adults in 1948 and 1960. *Connecticut State Department of Health, Office of Mental Retardation* (Hartford, Connecticut)

99. Skodak, M. (1968). In *Proceedings of the First Congress of the International*

Association for the Scientific Study of Mental Deficiency, Montpellier, France, 1967 (B. W. Richards, editor) (Reigate: Jackson)

100. Jensen, A. R. (1969). How much can we boost IQ in scholastic achievement? *Harvard Educ. Rev.*, **39**, 1

101. Heber, R. and Garber, H. (1972). In *Proceedings of the Second Congress of the International Association for the Scientific Study of Mental Deficiency, Warsaw, 1970,* (D. A. A. Primrose, editor) p. 31 (Warsaw: ARS Polona-Ruch, and Amsterdam: Swets and Zeitlinger)

102. Heber, R. and Garber, H. (1974). In D. A. A. Primrose (ed.). *Proceedings of the Third Congress of the International Association for the Scientific Study of Mental Deficiency, The Hague, 1973* (D. A. A. Primrose, editor) (Warsaw: ARS Polona-Ruch)

103. Hurowitz, I., Lloyd-Still, J. D., Wolff, P. H. and Shwachman, H. An item analysis of test performances of malnourished and control populations of children. (In preparation.)

CHAPTER 6

The social ecology of malnutrition in childhood*

CAROLYN MOORE NEWBERGER, ELI H. NEWBERGER
AND GORDON P. HARPER

INTRODUCTION

Nutritional problems reflect more than nutritional antecedents and require more than nutritional answers. Both to understand malnutrition, and to intervene, one must examine the setting in which it occurs. The forces which culminate in childhood nutritional problems may be seen at different levels of proximity to the child. Table 6.1 offers a framework for a discussion of the ecology of malnutrition in childhood at each of these various levels.

In this chapter illustrative examples are offered for each level of analysis. Representative cases demonstrate the economic, political, social and psychological factors involved in problems which present as nutritional deficiency in children.

ANALYSIS I: GIVEN THE PLANET EARTH, WHAT IS THE INTERNATIONAL AVAILABILITY OF FOOD RESOURCES?

During the past 3 years, the world has experienced a transition from a global food surplus to scarcity[1,2]. To be sure, some people, somewhere, have always been hungry. In the developing world according

* From the Judge Baker Guidance Center, Boston, Massachusetts, the Departments of Medicine and Psychiatry, Children's Hospital Medical Center, Boston, Massachusetts, and the Laboratory of Human Development and Departments of Pediatrics and Psychiatry, Harvard University. This work was supported in part by grants from the Danforth Foundation (CMN), the Office of Child Development, Department of Health, Education, and Welfare (EHN), and the Commonwealth Fund (GPH).

Table 6.1   A framework for an ecological analysis of malnutrition in childhood

Level of analysis	Given context	Relevant forces	Nutritional variable
I	The planet Earth	Realities of climate, population and soil; supply of energy and fertilizer; politics and balance of trade	International availability of nutritional resources
II	The international economic and political order	Social, political and economic order in a given country	Availability of food to family units
III	Social, political and economic order in a given country	Family functioning: stresses, distribution patterns, food beliefs, parental maturity, family size	Family ability to get food to the child
IV	A given family's way of functioning	Physical, social, cognitive, and psychological development of the child; health of the child	Child's ability to use what is available

to United Nations estimates about 50% of all young children may be inadequately nourished, which for many will lead inevitably to premature death. Approximately 30% of the total population in developing regions are suffering chronic, significant malnutrition[3]. But only recently has the coincidence of a total world food deficit and the increased agricultural interdependence among nations come to be widely acknowledged as the world food crisis. Several analyses of the crisis approach the ecology of factors affecting the food supply[4-6]. These analyses compel acknowledgement of a fundamental reality: climate, world economy and contemporary politics operate inevitably to promote the unequal and frequently inadequate distribution of nutritional resources.

The major factors in the growing global shortage of food are population growth, increasing affluence and changing patterns of food consumption in the industrialized world, falling cereal production due to adverse weather in several major regions of the world, Russia's decision to import vast quantities of grain to sustain livestock following major and erratic crop failures, and a fourfold increase between 1972 and 1974 in the cost of energy for fertilizer and irrigation[7]. An example of how the nutrition of nations is affected by events beyond their borders and control is offered by the experience of Sahelian West Africa during a recent 5-year drought.

Poor countries such as those stricken by the drought cannot produce a surplus of food even during the good years to carry them through bad ones. They are therefore extremely vulnerable to fluctuating weather conditions[8]. They must then compete for food in a world where several factors force increasing competition for food. Not only is world population increasing, and demanding to be fed, but the numbers of the affluent, who claim a disproportionate share of resources by consuming meat, an expensive and inefficient converter of grain, are rising as well. (5 pounds of grain protein are required to produce one pound of meat protein; beef and the fatter, more expensive grades of meat require even more[9].) On a *per capita* basis, people in the developed countries consume ten times as much grain, mostly in the form of meat, as those in the undeveloped countries[10]. Beef consumption is increasing, particularly in Europe, Russia and Japan[11]. If the average U.S. citizen were to reduce his consumption of meat by 10%, 12 million tons or more of grain would theoretically become available for purposes other than livestock production[12]. Thus, after the regional drought cut into West Africa's ability to feed itself, long-term developments in the rest of the world both reduced the supply and raised the price of grain for purchase and import. The extent of famine relief to West Africa, mostly from the U.S., was similarly limited by depletion of world grain reserves and the increased cost of food and transportation. Relief fell short of what was needed during the drought. A major factor in the recent depletion of reserves was the massive Russian purchase of American wheat in 1972. After poor wheat harvests in the early 1970s, instead of slaughtering and eating livestock as had been the practice during past grain shortages, the Soviet Union set out quietly to purchase much of the world's grain reserves[13]. The scale of the purchases involved led to world grain shortage and higher prices. (Farmers in the U.S., the main vendor, did not know of Russia's impending purchases; the major grain companies, who did, made enormous profits at the expense of farmers, and ultimately, of consumers[14].) Thus world grain reserves appear to have fed cattle rather than people.

The Soviet Union, which was able to purchase the grain with devalued dollars at prices subsidized by the United States Government, realized further profit, both economic and political, by selling, lending and granting of American grain to other countries. The extent to which Russia's refilling of Middle Eastern granaries with wheat from the United States encouraged the Arabs in 1972 is conjectural, but Mayer contends that it provided a critical economic underpinning for military action[15]. Thus ironically, world grain reserves which were grown primarily in the United States, fed Russian cattle and supported Russian, rather than American, political and financial interests. Moreover, because farmers in the U.S. did not free more land for cultivation until after the magnitude of the Russian purchases became known, the period of shortage and of higher prices was extended. This contributed to a substantial reduction in the amount of grain available for U.S. supported famine relief[16].

Famine relief, however, is not simply a matter of need, supply and altruism. The last decade offers several examples in addition to the Russian wheat sale of the use of food as an instrument of international politics. In 1973, the U.S., in its political and economic campaign against the Allende government in Chile, failed to respond to Chile's request for wheat on credit. This contributed to political instability and is believed to have accelerated the downfall of the Allende regime[17].

The destruction of food as a weapon of war has a long history, despite, as Mayer points out, its military inefficiency. Soldiers can generally procure what foodstuffs are available, while civilians suffer from starvation. 'Destruction of food never seems to hamper military operations, but always victimizes large numbers of children'[18]. Military destruction of agricultural capacity, as opposed to the destruction of current crops and reserves, inflicts more lasting damage, as first demonstrated by the Romans in salting the fields of conquered Carthage. In the Vietnam War, the latter-day counterpart of this policy, American widespread bombing, defoliation and crop destruction in North and South Vietnam, Laos and Cambodia, both depleted food supplies and rendered unproductive wide areas of previously fertile farmland. Extensive crop damage in the Vietnamese Highlands, for example, has led to displacement of a large segment of the indigenous population. The seriousness of the long-term consequences in Indochina are suggested by the estimate that 36–50% of the mangrove trees in Vietnam are destroyed, and under present conditions it may take over 100 years for the area to be reforested[19].

Once the current drought is past, West Africa's recovery and future ability to feed its population depend on the development of its agricultural potential, but its prospects for agricultural self-sufficiency seem poor. Higher food production in agriculturally underdeveloped areas requires intensive cultivation which in turn requires increased use of fertilizers[20, 21]. Yet with the fourfold rise in the price of oil, the investment required for fertilizer, pesticides and for energy for agriculture exceeds the rate of income growth among the world's poorest people[22]. In order to escape the cycle of drought and starvation, people who are getting poorer somehow have to obtain the energy needed for irrigation, fertilizer and personal strength. The price of the simplest fertilizer is drastically higher now that the oil-producing nations have increased the energy costs to produce it. This has made the green revolution financially inaccessible to poor farmers, on whose farms, ironically, fertilizer application yields the highest proportional return[23]. The world's limited supply of fertilizer is presently allocated according to ability to buy, rather than ability to use. Fertilizer's marginal utility is twice as great in the unenriched soil of poor nations as in the already rich soil of agriculturally developed countries. (Moreover, in addition to the forces of the marketplace, during the world fertilizer shortage of 1973, many of the principal exporter countries administratively restricted fertilizer exports to poor nations.)[24]

Even the 'limited supply' of fertilizer is not a fact of nature, but of the international economic and technological order. The huge amount of natural gas burned as waste in the oil-producing nations (more than three-fifths of the total world production) in 1972, could have been used as a raw material and as an energy source to provide twice the nitrogen fertilizer the world used in the same period. Its conversion on behalf of people, however, depends on those with the required technology (the U.S., Japan and Western Europe) and those with the gas[25, 26]. Although the United States has offered to build the plants to convert the gas to fertilizer, provided the fertilizer could be shipped at cost, the oil cartel has so far refused to co-operate[27].

Meanwhile, West African farmers unwittingly deplete their resources. Starving cattle (which in many traditional cultures are not kept for meat) overgraze the land, and the Sahara descends southward by 15–30 miles per year[28]. Traditional farming methods strip the land of many essential nutrients.

West Africa needs both capital and technology to enhance local productivity. Ironically, one finds here and elsewhere in the developing world vigorous promotion by major companies of products which actually lower, rather than raise the quality of diets: canned milk formula instead of breast milk, which is cheaper, better and safer for babies[29, 30]. Ross' foreign sales have expanded by more than 60% over the past 2 years, and critics maintain that the companies engage in promotional practices that are a powerful discouragement of breast feeding[31]. Meagre resources are squandered for products which degrade already inadequate diets[32].

Problems in the availability of food are thus seen to be related to distribution of agricultural resources, including climate, to the ratio of national income to population, and to the conditions under which food is traded. At the global level of analysis the following factors are relevant to change in nutritional status:

(1) rate of growth of world population;

(2) composition of diet of the affluent (there is much evidence to

suggest, furthermore, that such changes in diet as reducing consumption of meat and other foods rich in saturated fats would improve health, as well as reduce a disproportionate demand on a finite supply of grain);

(3) distribution of limited global resources, such as fertilizer;

(4) distribution of productive agricultural practices and technology. The world is increasingly dependent on food exports from North America and would be vulnerable were there to be an adverse climatic reversal there;

(5) readiness of the affluent nations to advance the principle that an adequate diet is a basic right of each individual, rather than an ingredient in the politics of food.

On the global level of analysis, national political and economic interests do not necessarily lead to international activity which promotes worldwide nutrition. Technical solutions—resource conservation, population stabilization, modern technology—will offer only partial solutions to the 'world food crisis'. The political ecology of malnutrition makes purely technical solutions inadequate and imposes a political and moral question: to what extent will the nations of the world agree to alter arrangements by which the unavailability of food continues to limit human development in much of the world?

ANALYSIS II: GIVEN THE INTERNATIONAL POLITICAL AND ECONOMIC ORDER, WHAT IS THE AVAILABILITY OF FOOD TO FAMILY UNITS?

The availability of food to individual family units in a particular country depends on the way the social, political and economic organization of that country furthers food production, distributes work, incomes and food, and differentially promotes food of different nutritional value.

Agricultural production may be organized in several forms. In Taiwan, for example, agricultural production quadrupled between 1911 and 1965, while population growth reduced average farm size from 5 to $2\frac{1}{2}$ acres. This was accomplished, not by the evolution of large-scale, highly mechanized farming, but on labour-intensive small farms. Labour-intensive farming has been the pattern in many countries, including Japan, Egypt, South Korea and Yugoslavia, which have achieved high per-acre yields on farms averaging 2–3 acres. This can only be achieved, however, when small rural farmers have access to such support systems as credit, health facilities, agricultural extension, transportation and marketing[33]. China has increased production to achieve self-sufficiency in food for its huge population, not through expensive, machine-based technology, but through nation-wide allocation of available resources and a decentralized pattern of agricultural development. More efficient land use is stressed, with use of improved seed, multiple cropping, increased fertilization and disease and insect control[34]. In these nations, national policy has encouraged an abundant labour force to cultivate limited land intensively, while providing supports both for agriculture and for rural life. Such labour-intensive farming promotes rural prosperity and full employment, thereby checking immigration to cities, as well as increasing production.

Other forms of agricultural organization, although productive of food, may be destructive of jobs. Technology which replaces labour will increase unemployment, income maldistribution and hunger, where the rest of the national economy is unable to absorb the idled workers. In Mexico, for example, agricultural production increased greatly during the 1960s, but worker-displacing mechanization, which largely accounted for the increase in agricultural productivity, swelled the number of landless workers by almost 50%, while their working days declined nearly by half. The incomes of labourers dropped as well, as agricultural mechanization eliminated jobs faster than industrial expansion created new ones[35]. The rise in unemployment swelled the city slums, as people migrated from the country in search of work.

Since World War II, the trend in the United States has also been toward the development of large, heavily mechanized family-owned farms and toward huge agricultural businesses ('agribusiness') which frequently control food production, processing, transportation and sales. Such vertical diversification and economics of scale make such units productive and successfully competitive: millions of small farmers have had to give up agriculture and move to urban areas, where they may have difficulty in finding jobs and adequately supporting their families[36]. (Walsh estimates that about 16% of the farms in the U.S. account for about 70% of farm income[37].)

Changes of this nature in such countries as the United States do not occur by historical accident. They derive from the economic and political policy of the country. In America, federal and state governments have supported the trend to large-unit agriculture. Agricultural corporate directors frequently punctuate their careers by serving in government posts which define agricultural policy[38]. Research monies are spent disproportionately to improve the efficiency of highly mechanized farming, frequently without consideration of nutritional values, such as the public investment in the development of hard tomatoes which can be picked quickly by machines rather than by hand[39, 40]. Government nutrition programmes, such as the surplus commodity distribution programme and the school lunch programmes, may have as primary goals the opening of markets for surplus commodities in order artificially to sustain their prices, rather than to foster the nutrition and health of the recipients. Butter and whole milk, for example, are staples of school lunch programmes, despite their known contribution to obesity and heart disease[41]. The wheat sale to Russia, while contributing to higher food prices for American consumers, profited five major grain companies (who, after the secret, subsidized sales, gave major contributions to the re-election campaign of the incumbent president)[42].

Many members of the American agricultural work-force displaced by agribusiness technology remain, in the absence of full employment or a full employment policy, unemployed and therefore at risk of malnutrition. At least 6% of the United States' population is estimated to suffer from clinical malnutrition[43]. In low income areas, the proportion is estimated to be higher. A ten-state survey conducted between 1968 and 1970 found that in the less affluent states 15.6% of whites, 37.4% of blacks and 20.6% of Spanish Americans had evidence of malnutrition[44]. With inflation, the situation appears to be worsening[45].

Programmes to supplement nutritionally inadequate diets in the United States have not been successful in eliminating malnutrition. The Food Stamp Programme, for example, is intended to meet the nutritional needs of the poor. But in 1974, only 35.6% of those eligible for the programme were enrolled. Several reasons have been cited. For the poorest people in the United States even the cost of food stamps is more than they can afford[46]. Furthermore, federal programmes, locally administered, become subject to local politics. Counties must request Food Stamp Programmes, and the United States Department of Agriculture is reluctant to override local authority, so that many poor people cannot obtain food stamps simply because their local governments choose not to adopt the programme. Even when adopted, in some rural counties food programmes are suspended during harvest seasons to guarantee a supply of cheap labour[47]. In addition, inconvenient hours, bureaucratic red tape, office locations which are not accessible by public transportation and a lack of information about the programmes, discourage participation[48]. Even with the stamps, data from the United States Department of Agriculture indicate that many families still cannot purchase a nutritionally adequate diet[49].

In countries, in short, where food is allocated according to purchasing power, hunger and malnutrition are concentrated among the poor. Other allocation systems may be used in wartime, when minimal food needs are guaranteed to all by rationing, and extra allotments go to those with special health needs or to support strenuous work[50]. In peace, such allocation may be made for certain groups (children, for example) who are felt to have needs which take priority. In Cuba, as part of a larger redistribution of resources, scarce essential foods like milk and meat have been rationed in peacetime, again with priority to children and to pregnant or nursing mothers. Depite much documentation both of malnutrition and of the possibilities for dietary enrichment in the rest of Latin America, including nearby Central America, the Cuban precedent (which began without benefit of nutritional study) has yet to be generalized.

In the United States, in addition to those barriers to nutrition arising from income disparity and a system of allocation based on wealth, a food industry seeking innovative accesses to profitable markets erects other barriers to good nutrition. With slow population growth and declining food consumption due to a more sedentary life-style, industry is turning increasingly toward the development of highly processed, more expensive and less nutritious 'convenience' foods. The percentage of processed foods in the American diet has risen from 10% in 1941 to 50% in 1971. To some extent the nutritional inadequacy of such foods has been compensated by the fortification of flour-based foods with vitamins and iron. Yet, advertising presses for increased consumption of the least valuable foods (snacks, candy, soft drinks, sugared breakfast cereals) and 'is threatening to destroy family eating habits'[51].

French Sahelian Africa offers an example of how national economic and social policy may indirectly affect nutrition. A policy of assuring jobs to all secondary school graduates has created a swollen and un-productive civil service and an ensuing budgetary crisis in several countries. In order to hold down the salaries of civil service employees, several governments have had to resort to a policy of controlling the price of food, for example, by keeping prices of such grain staples as millet at about one-half of what they would be in a free market situation. Such policy makes it unprofitable for many farmers to grow more than they and their families need, perhaps contributing in part to the devastating effects of the drought on people whose grain reserves are limited, and who have little capital with which to purchase grain and other foodstuffs at times of crisis[52].

In the level II analysis, we have seen how applied technology and increased production *per se* do not necessarily benefit all, or even most, of certain populations. The social, political and economic order, on a national level determine whether and how families are fed.

ANALYSIS III: GIVEN THE ORGANIZATION OF A PARTICULAR COUNTRY'S ECONOMIC AND SOCIAL POLICIES, WHAT IS THE FAMILY'S ABILITY TO NOURISH ITS CHILDREN?

Many factors influence a family's capacity to feed and nourish its children. Most important, in societies where access to food depends on wealth, is income distribution. This analysis will explore how forces on the level of the family itself limit its ability to deliver to its children the food resources which the economic and social order make available to the family. Within the ceiling imposed by income, such family factors as customs, education, values and intercurrent stress are all clearly relevant[53, 54].

As a clinical illustration of the effect of such factors on the nutritional status of the child, failure to thrive may be considered. This illness of infants and young children is defined by a serious failure to attain expected height and weight in the absence of demonstrable organic causes.

It has been argued that the antecedents of failure to thrive are primarily nutritional. Whitten conducted an experiment in which children admitted to hospital with failure to thrive were allocated to two groups, one fed and stimulated, the other fed and unstimulated. Comparable weight gain in both groups led to the conclusions that availability of food was the effective therapy and, further, that *un-availability* of food had been the effective cause of the illness[55]. Such logic ignored the first step in intervention, which had been *removal* of the children from the home setting and the *provision* of stable relationships in hospital.

Other authors have focused on the family setting of failure to thrive[56-58]. In this perspective, failure to thrive may be considered as

Table 6.2 CHMC Study of pediatric social illness: a priori stress-strength scales, means for inpatient groups*

	Stress in mother's childhood	Stress in current household	Lack of social support
Inpatient			
Accident	0.04	0.59*	0.19
Ingestion	0.46*	0.34	0.15
Failure to thrive	0.47*	0.27	0.52*
Abuse	1.15*	1.58*	0.83*

standardized to mean and S. D. of controls

* $P < 0.01$ by one-tailed t test

one of a group of pediatric 'social illnesses' (accidents, poisonings and child abuse and neglect as well as failure to thrive) which appear to have similar social and environmental origins[59-61]. Data from the Family Development Study, a large, controlled descriptive epidemiological inquiry into the postulated common origins of the early childhood 'social illnesses', indicate certain common features among them[62]. (Data for the study came from detailed, closed-ended interview schedules administered by trained interviewers to a population matched for social class, ethnic status and age of child.) Table 6.2 summarizes findings with regard to stress in mother's childhood, stress in the current household, and lack of social support. The forty-two failure to thrive cases in this series differed significantly from the controls in the first and latter scales, stress in mother's childhood and lack of social support.

The data suggest that definable ecological forces affect the family's *capacity to nurture its offspring.* Failure to thrive, then, can be seen as a nutritional consequence of earlier parental experience and lack of current social supports. The following case describes how such experiences were expressed in a growth problem in a child and how the child responded to intervention which filled some of the gaps in current social supports.

A ten-month-old black female entered the hospital for the second time. Her first admission was at 8 months for evaluation of weight loss. The second admission was for physical neglect and continued low weight.

The child was born at term, with birth weight 2.85 kg. Delivery and perinatal period were unremarkable. At home, the child was said to be a quiet baby, and her mother reported that she was worried at first that the baby did not move her legs enough. She said, 'I was sure there was something wrong with her.' Reports of early vomiting and poor sucking led to a change from a prepared formula to an evaporated milk-corn syrup preparation which was well tolerated. Cereal and canned juices were added at about 1 month; mashed beef, vegetables, banana and potato at 3 months. At the time of admission she was said to be offered food three times a day and to be taking chicken, noodles, peaches, vegetables and other table foods. She had no history of vomiting or diarrhea. Developmental milestones were delayed: she could neither sit up nor maintain a sitting position. She was said not to vocalize in response to social stimulation.

On examination, she was a small, emaciated child who did not respond to play. Her length was 62 cm, weight 3.95 kg and head circumference 38.5 cm. These growth parameters were well below the third percentile of the normal distributions for children her age. Physical neglect was evidence by a general macular-papular rash over her upper chest, hands and arms; dry and scaly skin with cracks over the knuckles and between the fingers, which she sucked constantly; and moderate hip and elbow contractures. Skeletal X-rays showed a bone age of 5 months and all laboratory analyses were normal.

The family did not have a history of short stature. The mother was unmarried, and this was the fourth child of a fourth father.

The mother was one of seven children born and raised in North Carolina. Both her parents were seriously ill. She first came to Boston in her early twenties with a cousin and worked for a year as a domestic. She then left work, due in part to her pregnancy with her first child, who was 4 years of age at the time of the patient's admission. In Boston, the family had few friends or relatives, and the mother suffered from constantly aching teeth.

The mother and her children were supported by public welfare, with approximately half the monthly stipend ($115) going for rent. Although a home visit revealed a spacious, clean and well kept apartment, the mother described a life copattern nsistent with family disorganization: all members of the household slept until noon and stayed up until one to two in the morning; meals were at irregular times.

While at first the mother appeared slow to grasp instructions, on further contact it became clear that she had adequate intellectual understanding of her problems. Yet she could muster little energy to care for her children. Although the mother was appreciated to be depressed and isolated, treatment was focused on the child.

The baby was given a regular diet with an average daily intake of 250 calories/kg. She promptly gained weight, started to smile and to demonstrate interest in people who played with her. Physical therapy mobilized her stiff elbows and hips. She was soon sent home with only routine follow-up in medical out-patient department.

On readmission 2 months later, she was a small, dirty, smelly infant, active with restless movements of her hands, and again underweight.

While the child again responded to re-feeding, appreciation of the mother's depression and her many problems, including untreated health problems (carious teeth and chronic urinary tract infection) led to a different form of intervention. She was seen to have been overwhelmed by stress and unable to provide for her baby's needs. Practical and emotional support was offered: dental and medical care for the mother, regular counselling with a social worker, and child care for the older two children. As her depression lifted and her capacity to provide the child's needs for stimulation, love, and care appeared to improve, the child was sent home for progressively longer visits. After discharge, in addition to the efforts already under way, follow-up care included a home-maker and a public health nurse for day-to-day support. The child continued to gain weight at home, and 4 years later, at the age of 5, her physical and psychological growth are in the normal range.

This case of failure to thrive could be approached from many different perspectives. From the history one can surmise that events on the national, state and city level shaped the mother's move from North Carolina to Boston, the straitened material circumstances of their life, and the irregularity of their medical care. Similarly, on an individual level, her own early experiences, limited education, social and personal isolation, and susceptibility to depression can be cited. Her feelings toward this pregnancy and the child she feared couldn't be normal remain unexplored. And within the child, the possibility that constitutional activity level contributed to a 'temperamental mismatch' between child and parent cannot be excluded.

But medical care in this case focused on an intermediate variable—a family which had stopped functioning. Intervention took the form of providing social supports to help the family resume functioning and was gratifyingly effective. By acting on the cause of despair—the loneliness, the aching teeth, the failing baby—and so demonstrating that solutions exist for troubles, the clinicians helped the family begin to cope. The family is now able to manage the tasks of living and nurture its children despite the fact that the larger social and economic reality, and the mother's own early history, could not be changed.

It is well to underline certain clinical features of this case. There were *early* symptoms of trouble in the mother-child dyad, manifest in the parent's concern about whether the child was normal and in the neonatal feeding difficulties. Klaus and Kennell have drawn attention to the critical importance of the newborn period in establishing an enduring maternal-infant bond[63]. On the first hospital admission for failure to thrive, there were both physical and developmental signs of inadequate care in weight, length, socialization, hygiene and hip and elbow immobility. Her discharge from hospital was, in retrospect, premature.

When the child was admitted the second time bearing signs of neglect, there was more comprehensive response from the medical staff.

Although it is easier in many such cases to separate the child from its family, the psychological cost for the child and the financial impact for society of this practice are considerable[64]. The anger aroused by such cases, however, often leads clinicians to look for someone to blame. A punitive approach to parents is implied by simple diagnostic formulations such as 'parental failure', 'maternal deprivation' and the 'battered child syndrome'[65, 66]. Ryan has aptly characterized such an approach to parental problems as 'blaming the victim'[67]. Identifying those aspects of the mother's social, physical and psychological context which undermined her ability to care for her children, and which could be practically addressed by the individuals in the setting to which she came for help, was the primary task to inform intervention, not judgement or blame, and not superficial approaches to symptom reduction in the child.

Such cases demand flexibility, understanding and creativity in clinical diagnosis and treatment, and they frequently pose formidable ethical, technical and organizational challenges[68].

Failure to thrive is but one of many childhood nutritional problems which warrant addressing the family setting. Other examples include: the family in an underdeveloped country which abandons breastfeeding and feeds its baby a bottle in response to familial, cultural and promotional pressures to be modern[69, 70]; the family in traditional cultures where the father has first access to protein-rich foods, rendering the children early victims should shortage occur[71]; poor single-parent families where working mothers cannot be home and cannot afford babysitters to assure that their children are fed; the family in an industrialized society, in which a working mother turns to nutrient-deficient convenience foods because she does not have time or energy to prepare inexpensive, time consuming, but more nutritious meals; and the affluent families whose children do not sit down to nutritious, well-balanced meals, but grab bologna, soda pop and potato chips from cupboard and refrigerator.

In analysis III, at the level of individual children in particular families, an understanding of how the family organizes itself around food and feeding is critical to an understanding of many nutritional problems. And intervention on behalf of the family, rather than narrowly in terms of the nutrition of the child, is often essential to effect enduring nutritional change.

ANALYSIS IV: GIVEN A FAMILY'S WAY OF FUNCTIONING, WHAT IS THE CHILD'S CONTRIBUTION TO HIS OWN NUTRITION?

The fourth level at which the ecology of malnutrition in childhood may be considered is that of forces operating within the child. On this level of analysis, the features of a family are taken as given, for better or worse, and the relevant variables are viewed from the standpoint of the child alone. These variables interact, to be sure, with those on all the previous levels, especially with those in the family, but we restrict our perspective here, for purposes of exposition, to those forces in the child himself.

Physiological factors in the child which produce malnutrition include central nervous system disease affecting *appetite*; inadequate *assimilation* of food in diseases involving malabsorption; increased metabolic *requirements* found with fever, infections or malignancy; *loss* of food in vomiting or diarrhea of any aetiology; and metabolic *defects* found in some storage diseases, aminoacidopathies and disturbed metabolic states[72].

When such factors operate alone, they present little problem for understanding their nutritional implications. But when physiological disorders in the child *interact* with the child's *emotional development*, or when *psychological* complications of disease dominate the picture, the illness may be considered a more complicated 'psycho-nutritional' syndrome. Such syndromes are those of 'non-organic failure to thrive' in infancy and toddlers; oppositional eating disorders in toddlers and older children; depressive syndromes in toddlers and older children; and anorexia nervosa and emotional–nutritional complications of chronic illness such as diabetes mellitus, occurring primarily in adolescence.

Understanding any of these syndromes requires consideration of the *child's* contribution to malnutrition. This requires examination of the psychological development of the child[73].

Eating involves co-ordinating physiological and psychological needs with the aliments, schedules and relationships available outside. The figurative psychological 'organ' of the personality which integrates all of these and co-ordinates responses to the environment is the *ego*. Disorders in which a child participates in his own malnutrition represent, accordingly, a serious derailment of the ego's work.

Erikson has described the growth of the ego in terms of a sequence of *basic strengths* which emerge at each stage of the life cycle and which comprise the resources of the functioning ego[74]. We borrow on his formulation in reviewing the contributions of factors *in* the child to nutritional disorders.

We stress at the outset how different is this perspective, dealing with forces acting *within* the child, from that usually used in discussing 'non-organic' malnutrition or growth failure. Such syndromes are customarily thought to result from 'deprivation', meaning maternal deprivation. The term 'deprivational dwarfism', for example, has been used to refer to environmentally-related growth failure. (Rutter has outlined the problems with uncritical use of the concept of 'deprivation')[75]. 'Deprivation' is often used, moreover, to suggest that the relevant interactions are all one way: the depriving parent acting on the passive child. A review of development from the child's point of view indicates that his is quite active, and increasingly so, in the interactions involved in his nutrition.

In infancy, a mutually satisfying relationship in which his needs for food and care are consistently met supports the development in the child of an inner sense that he can rely on the world to meet his needs, that he can manage those needs himself within the framework of the caregivers' responses, and that he can trust himself not to drive away with his neediness those on whom he relies for the satisfaction of those needs. This inner sense is called Basic Trust. The syndromes of infantile 'non-organic' malnutrition, namely *failure to thrive* and *rumination*, have consistently been observed to occur in settings in which such a relationship did not exist or was lost.[76-79]. The infant's *active withdrawal* from all relationships, including eating, could be observed. The polar sense to Basic Trust, Basic Mistrust, which exists alongside the positive sense throughout life, could be said to have become dominant.

It has become an axiom of the clinical management of these syndromes that some *re-establishment of a trusting relationship* is a prerequisite for clinical recovery. This may occur in hospitals or in a home, either with surrogate parents or with the natural parents. In hospital the provision of this relationship often takes the form of assigning a special nurse to the child, instead of the usual hospital pattern of staff rotation. Work with the child's parents takes the form, as outlined in the preceding section, of meeting *their* needs to the point where they themselves feel able to care for the child.

Discussion of Basic Trust as an inner sense accruing during infancy should not give the impression of a once-for-all psychological 'achievement'. The ratio of Basic Trust to Basic Mistrust with which a given infant emerges from infancy is a dynamic ratio, affected by the events in the world around him currently as well as by his past experiences. The reaction of the child to loss of a care-giver (or care-giving situation) has been called *anaclitic depression*[80]. Depressive syndromes with despondency, anorexia and weight loss occur in children and adults alike following losses of severe degree.

The taxonomy, postulated aetiologies and treatment of depressive phenomena in adults are not directly applicable to childhood. Yet the existence of syndromes in children in which emotional despair, behavioural withdrawal, physiological anorexia and physical weight loss occur is clear. With or without the appearance of frank malnutrition the illness may be life-threatening. Effective treatment requires careful attention to the life events, the emotional life and the behavioural characteristics of these children[81].

The second basic strength or ego quality involved in eating is the sense of one's personal control of what, where, when, with whom and how fast one is going to eat. While this quality begins to develop during infancy and continues to be an issue throughout life, it becomes a focus of development between the second half of the first and the third year of life. This quality is usefully called *Autonomy*, and is contrasted with the polar sense of Shame and Doubt. Determination in making choices, and aggressive wishes to control others as well as oneself must be integrated into the personality during this period. In children whose attempts to develop autonomy are frustrated, oppositional behaviour, frequently around eating, may appear[82]. Such behaviour is familiar to parents of two-year-olds and is a normal part of a child's learning to do things on his own and to manage his will in co-ordination with others. In particularly unfavourable situations where the development of autonomy is unduly frustrated, oppositional behaviour (or undue compliance) can take on pathological proportions and can become a more lasting personality feature.

The following case illustrates a child's participation in an oppositional eating disorder which led to growth arrest. It outlines the *forces in him* which sustained the pathological pattern and indicates the elements of a successful intervention programme.

> An 8 4/12-year-old white male was admitted to hospital for evaluation of short stature and an unusual feeding disorder: a craving, unmanageable in the home, for foods to which he was thought to be allergic.
>
> His history included an unremarkable pregnancy and delivery, with birth weight of 3.3 kg, an apparent milk allergy from early infancy, which led to his being fed a milk-free formula, and retarded growth, both in height and weight, from the 2nd year. Parents were of average height. His motor and linguistic development were unremarkable. Clinical investigation at two hospitals did not support the parents' continuing belief that food allergy in this 'sickly' child accounted for his short stature; physicians could point to no specific cause for the growth failure. Oppositional behaviour in the home around eating seemed a more likely factor. He picked at meals (while parents tried to make him eat), then made nightly raids on the refrigerator (which the parents tried, ineffectively, to lock), gorged on foods such as mustard and chocolate, then woke mother and vomited. It was the *way* he ate (in a larger sense the way the family fed him and he ate), rather than *what* he ate, that was stunting his growth. He had become a babyish child, scapegoated by his peers.
>
> On admission the patient's height and weight were appropriate for an average $4\frac{1}{2}$-year-old; he had not gained any weight in a year, nor height in 6 months. Aside from his stature, he lacked physical and biochemical stigmata of malnutrition. Behaviourally, he alternated between clinging and whining, like a younger child, and subtle provocation of other children, resulting in his being scapegoated. At meals he dawdled, took large portions and did not eat them, and got up and walked around the dining-room. In his play and fantasy he showed fears of his own assertiveness. Frustrated in developing autonomy, he seemed always to be looking,

but in self-defeating ways, for outer controls. His family's responses (such as dictating what he could eat or locking the refrigerator), only confirmed his unconscious identity as one incapable of inner controls.

Treatment offered him a chance, in the milieu with other children, and in play therapy, to experiment with his own assertiveness and to see that he could make choices autonomously and without endangering himself or others. His parents had the opportunity in social casework to review sympathetically the issues in their lives which had made this child hard to care for, and to appreciate the ways that they could foster, rather than always locking horns with, his attempts to do things for himself.

During a $2\frac{1}{2}$ months' hospitalization, he began eating, appropriately and even (for the first time in his life) with gusto, and resumed growth. He eventually closed between one-third and one-half of the large gap between his retarded growth progression and the third percentile for his age. This pattern continued after discharge. There was no vomiting, regardless of what he ate. Marked gains occurred in peer relations and in school behaviour and work.

The parents were particularly pleased to be able to enjoy activities with this child, rather than finding themselves always engaged in an oppositional struggle with him. The major casualties of that struggle had been his growth and their mutual enjoyment of each other.

The third developmental period in which children are particularly vulnerable to eating disorders and nutritional disturbance is adolescence. During this time youths are wrestling with issues of separating from parents, integrating their own sexuality (or the prospect of it), and so consolidating the formation of their own *Identity*.

Such adolescent issues are generally assumed to underlie a serious disorder of nutrition, anorexia nervosa or self-starvation, which can occur from the years of pre-adolescence through young adulthood, but is most common in the mid and late teenage years. The particular psychological issues in given patients may vary, that is, self-starvation may be a 'final common pathway' with various approach routes according to each individual's own situation. Observers positing different dynamic determinants agree, however, that anorexia nervosa is a massive 'holding action' in which the body is made to serve the psychological need of slowing down development, when growing up appears foreboding, impossible to manage, or lethal[83, 84]. The words of Marlowe's Faustus as the designated hour of his doom approached, 'Lente lente currite noctis equi' (Go slow, go slow, ye racing steeds of night) epitomize the wish of this group of patients to see developmental time stop.

For many patients, treatment requires separation from the home environment in which the impasse has arisen and benignly taking over the feeding function. Clinicians must help the child (and family) gradually unravel the developmental knot in which they have become entangled. Behavioural therapies have been promoted recently in this disorder, with some demonstration of efficacy and rapid recovery, but Bruch has warned that such approaches, if they focus only on the weight disorder and ignore the psychological issues, are unwise and potentially dangerous[85].

Other nutritional manifestations of the emotional changes of adolescence can be seen in children with diabetes mellitus, in which treatment involves both dietary management and the use of insulin. Many adolescents, even those with 'good adjustments' to the illness in pre-adolescence, 'reject' their illness, emotionally and practically. They seem to need to repudiate and then reappropriate, on their own terms, such a major part of themselves as a chronic illness. The denial, bargaining, anger and sadness involved can be seen as a kind of mourning process for the intact body they freshly realize, in adolescence, they do not have. This integration of the illness on an individual level is a part of identity formation. It is, of course, complicated by identity problems arising in other parts of life and by despair about the child or the illness on the part of the family.

At Level IV of the analysis of the social ecology of malnutrition in childhood, the child's own contribution to his nutrition has been considered. At particular points in development, eating normally becomes a focus for the expression of developmental issues. This section has described how children may respond to interpersonal, physical and psychological stress, particularly during developmentally vulnerable periods, by compromising their own nutritional intake. As the case example illustrates, it is to be emphasized that each child's problem needs to be understood in its family context.

CONCLUSION

This chapter has presented a four-level framework for understanding childhood malnutrition in context. Each level of analysis can ultimately be related to the individual child. For example, the ability of the family in Analysis III to get food to the child was compromised by factors operating at each level of analysis. Global and national events and policies contributed to agricultural mechanization and displacement of the rural work force in the South, and to the chronic unemployment and to the lack of resources for the reconstruction of family life in the North. Although poverty contributed to the child's malnutrition, poverty *per se* did not cause the failure to thrive. Rather, stresses associated with poverty intensified the mother's own psychological and physical vulnerability and compromised her ability to nurture and to nourish her child. The child became ill at an age when her major developmental need was for a consistent, mutually satisfying relationship with a care-giver, a relationship of which her ill and depressed mother was not capable. To the extent that the mother's perception of the baby as abnormally quiet and probably defective, in part a reflection of the apathy of early failure to thrive and in part a projection onto the baby of the mother's own sense of worthlessness, was also a reflection of the baby's constitutional temperament, factors intrinsic to the child herself contributed to the illness.

The usefulness of a more proximal (individual or familial) as opposed to a more distant (national or global) level of analysis is determined by the role in which one is able or chooses to address the problem. In the above case, although all levels of analysis can be seen to bear on the nutritional outcome in the child, clinical intervention occurred on Level III, directly within the family system and enabled the family and the child to 'recover'. On the other hand, the prevalence of iron deficiency anaemia among poor children in the United States, or of marasmus in India and West Africa is unarguably a direct result of poverty, and requires analysis and intervention on the level of the social, economic and political organization of the given country which allows some children to be malnourished while others thrive.

We have presented a model which identifies and clarifies relationships among many phenomena which bear on childhood malnutrition. Different determinants operate on the nutrition ecosystem at different levels, and they require appropriate perspectives for understanding and strategies for intervention.

REFERENCES

1. Brown, L. and Eckholm, E. (1974). *By Bread Alone.* p. 3 (New York: Praeger)
2. Revelle, R. (1974). Food and population. *Scientific American*, **231**, 161
3. Food and Agriculture Organization of the United Nations (1974). *The State of Food and Agriculture*, p. 107 (Rome: FAO)
4. Brown, L. and Eckholm, E. *op. cit.*
5. Borgstrom, G. (1974). *The Food/People Dilemma.* (Duxbury Press)
6. Lerza, C. and Jacobson, M. (1975). *Food for People, Not for Profit.* A Sourcebook on the Food Crisis. (New York: Ballantine Books)
7. Mayer, J. (1975). Is the World's Worst Famine Coming? Presented at the Cambridge Forum, January 8, Cambridge, Massachusetts
8. Revelle, R. *op. cit.*
9. Berg, A. (1973). *The Nutrition Factor*, p. 65. (Washington, D.C.: The Brookings Institution)
10. Poleman, T. (1975). World food: a perspective. *Science*, **188**, 510
11. Revelle, R. *op. cit.*
12. Brown, L. and Eckholm, E. *op. cit.* p. 206
13. Lerza, C. and Jacobson, M. *op. cit.* p. 3
14. Krebs, A. V. (1975). Of the Grain Trade, by the Grain Trade, and for the Grain Trade. In *Food for People, Not for Profit.* (C. Lerza and M. Jacobson, editors) p. 353 (New York: Ballantine Books)
15. Mayer, A. and Mayer, J. (1974). Agriculture, the island empire. *Daedalus*, **103**, 83
16. *Ibid.*
17. Brown, L. and Eckholm, E. *op. cit.* p. 69
18. Mayer, J. (1972). *Human Nutrition.* Its Physiological, Medical and Social Aspects. A Series of Eighty-Two Essays. p. 681 (Springfield: Charles Thomas)
19. Constable, J. D., Cook, R. E., Meselson, M. AAAS and NAS Herbicide Reports (1974). *Science*, **186**, 584
20. Myrdal, G. (1974). The transfer of technology to underdeveloped countries. *Scientific American*, **231**, 173
21. Grant, J. (1973). A New Development Policy. In *Food for People, Not for Profit.* (C. Lerza and M. Jacobson, editors) p. 253. (New York: Ballantine Books)
22. Brown, L. and Eckholm, E. *op. cit.* p. 12

23. Food and Agriculture Organization of the United Nations. *op. cit.* pp. 28–30
24. Walters, H. (1975). Difficult issues underlying food problems. *Science,* **188**, 524
25. Mayer, J. (1975) *op. cit.*
26. Brown, L. and Eckholm, E. (1974). *op. cit.* p. 113
27. Mayer, J. (1975) *op. cit.*
28. Brown, L. and Eckholm, E. (1974) *op. cit.* p. 10
29. Editorial (1975) *Lancet,* **ii**, 313
30. Wade, N. (1974). Bottle feeding: adverse effects of a western technology. *Science,* **184**, 45
31. Crittenden, A. (1975). Baby formula sales in third world are criticized. *The New York Times,* September 11, 1975
32. Lenza, C. and Jacobson, M. *op. cit.* p. 5
33. Grant, J. *op. cit.*
34. Sprague, G. F. (1975). Agriculture in China. *Science,* **188**, 549
35. Grant, J. *op. cit.*
36. Walsh, J. (1975). U.S. Agribusiness and agricultural trends. *Science,* **188**, 531
37. *Ibid.*
38. Jacobson, Michael and White, Robert. (1973). Company Town at FDA. In *Food for People, Not for Profit.* (C. Lerza and M. Jacobson, editors) (1975). p. 372 (New York: Ballantine Books)
39. Hightower, J. and deMarco, S. (1972) Hard Tomatoes, Hard Times. In *Food for People, Not for Profit* (C. Lerza and M. Jacobson, editors) (1975) p. 389
40. Mayer, A. and Mayer, J. (1974). *op. cit.*
41. Mayer, J. (1972) *op. cit.* p. 612
42. Krebs, A. V. *op. cit.*
43. Brown, L. and Eckholm, E. (1975) *op. cit.* p. 33
44. Carter, J. (1974). *The Ten-State Nutrition Survey: An Analysis.* (Atlanta, Georgia: Southern Regional Council, Inc.)
45. Robbins, W. (1974). The American food scandal. *The New York Times,* October 29, 1974
46. Pollack, R. (1975). The Poor Pay More. In C. Lerza and M. Jacobson (eds) *op. cit.* p. 305
47. Mayer, J. (1972) *op. cit.* p. 637
48. Greenstein, R. (1975) An End to Persistent Poverty and Hunger in America. In C. Lerza and M. Jacobson *op. cit.* p. 311
49. *Ibid.*
50. Dwyer, J. T. and Mayer, J. (1975). Beyond economics and nutrition: the complex basis of food policy. *Science,* **188**, 557
51. Mayer, J. (1972). *op. cit.* p. viii
52. Sanderson, F. H. (1975). The great food fumble. *Science,* **188**, 503
53. Richardson, S. A. (1968). The Influence of Social, Environmental and

Nutritional Factors on Mental Ability. In *Malnutrition, Learning and Behavior.* (N. S. Scrimshaw and J. E. Gordon, editors) p. 346. (Cambridge, Massachusetts: MIT Press)

54. Gordon, J. E. (1975). Nutritional individuality. *Am. J. Dis. Childh.*, **129**, 422

55. Whitten, C. F. (1969). Evidence that growth failure from malnutrition is secondary to understanding. *J. Am. Med. Ass.*, **209**, 1675

56. Glaser, H. H., *et al.* (1968). Physical and psychological development of children with early failure to thrive. *J. Pediatr.*, **73**, 690

57. Barbero, G. J. and Shaheen, E. (1967). Environmental failure to thrive: A clinical view. *J. Pediatr.*, **71**, 639

58. Talbot, N. B., Kagan, J. and Eisenberg, L. (1971). *Behavioral Science in Pediatric Medicine.* (London and Toronto: W. B. Saunders Co.)

59. Bullard, D. M., Glaser, H. H., Heagarty, M. C. and Pivchik, E. C. (1967). Failure to thrive in the neglected child. *Am. J. Orthopsychiatry*, **37**, 680

60. Koel, B. S. (1969). Failure to thrive and fatal injury as a continuum. *Am. J. Dis. Childh.*, **118**, 565

61. Newberger, E. H. *et al.* (1975). Toward an etiologic classification of pediatric social illness: A descriptive epidemiology of child abuse and neglect, failure to thrive, accidents and poisonings in children under four years of age. Presented at the *Biennial Meeting of the Society for Research in Child Development*, April 11, 1975, Denver, Colorado

62. *Ibid.*

63. Klause, M. and Kennell, J. (1972). Maternal attachment: Importance of the first post-partum days. *N. Eng. J. Med*, **186**, 460

64. Fanschel, D. and Shinn, E. B. (1972). *Dollars and Sense in the Foster Care of Children: A Look at Cost Factors.* (New York: Child Welfare League of America)

65. Newberger, E. (1973). The myth of the battered child syndrome. *Current Medical Dialogue*, **xxxx**, 327

66. Newberger, C., and Newberger, E. (1975). Inadequate mothers. *Lancet*, **i**, 42

67. Ryan, W. (1971). *Blaming the Victim.* (New York: Pantheon)

68. Newberger, E. H. and Hyde, J. N., Jr. (1975). Child Abuse: Principles and implications of current practice. *Pediatric Clinics of North America*, **22**, 695

69. Wade, N. (1974). *op. cit.*

70. Berg, A. (1973) *op. cit.* p. 99

71. *Ibid*, p. 46

72. Green, M. and Richmond, J. B. (1954). *Pediatric Diagnosis.* 206. (Philadelphia: Saunders)

73. Newberger, E. H. and Howard, R. (1973). A conceptual approach to the child with exceptional nutritional requirements. *Clin. Pediatr.*, **12**, 456

74. Erikson, E. H. (1963). *Childhood and Society* (New York: Norton)

75. Rutter, M. (1972). *Maternal Deprivation Reassessed.* (Baltimore: Penguin)

76. Talbot, N. B., Sobel, E. H., Burke, B. S., Lindemann, E., and S. B Kaufman. (1947). Dwarfism in healthy children: Its possible relation to emotional, nutritional and endocrine disturbances. *N Engl. J. Med.,* **236,** 783
77. Powell, G. F., J. A. Brasel, and R. M. Blizzard. (1967). Emotional deprivation and growth retardation simulating idiopathic hypopituitarism. I. Clinical evaluation of the syndrome. *N Engl. J. Med.,* **276,** 1271
78. Patton, R. G., and L. I. Gardner. (1962). *Growth Failure in Materna Deprivation.* (Springfield: Charles C. Thomas)
79. Richmond, J. B., Eddy, E. F. and Green, M. (1958). Rumination, psychosomatic syndrome of infancy. *Pediatrics.,* **22,** 49
80. Spitz, R. and Wolf, K. M. (1946). Anaclitic depression: An inquiry into the genesis of psychiatric conditions in early childhood. *Psychoanal. Stud. Child.,* **2,** 313
81. Malmquist, C. P. (1971). Depression in childhood and adolescence. *N Engl. J. Med.,* **284,** 887 and 955
82. Crisp, A. H. (1970). Anorexia nervosa: 'Feeding disorder,' 'nervous malnutrition', or 'weight phobia'. *World Rev. Nutr. Diets,* **12,** 452
83. Galdston, R. (1974) Mind over Matter: Observations on fifty patients hospitalized with anorexia nervosa. *J. Am. Acad. Child Psychiat.,* **13,** 264
84. Bruch, H. (1974). Perils of behavior modification in treatment of anorexia nervosa. *J. Am. Med. Ass.,* **230,** 1419

Index